MORE PRAISE for *The 8 Keys to End Bullying Activity Program for Kids & Tweens*

"Well-organized and easily relatable, this workbook and companion guide will help kids understand categories of aggressive behaviors—such as how rude, mean, and bullying behaviors differ—and teach them to treat others with respect and kindness. Bravo for a fun, accessible anti-bullying activity program!"

—**Carrie Goldman**, award-winning author of *Bullied: What Every Parent, Teacher, and Kid Needs to Know About Ending the Cycle of Fear*

"Signe Whitson continues to provide value that very few do: a detailed approach that offers tools and skill-building for young people in an action-based training format. This is the only way to impact one of our toughest issues that all people face: bullying. An amazing resource for educators and parents, with proven strategies to fight bullying situations."

—**Jason Spector**, Veteran Physical Educator and Coach, Co-Founder of Sweethearts and Heroes Anti-Bullying Program, father of two

"Signe Whitson continues to be one of the most dynamic leaders in bullying education and crisis intervention among youth. These interactive guides for students, parents, and educators provide the hands-on tools to help kids and tweens cope wisely with real-life situations, both offline and online. These workbooks are full of engaging and collaborative games, worksheets, and thought-provoking activities that will stay with your child longer than simply reading a book. Whitson's activity program allows you to get involved with your child on both an emotional level and an educational one—these are definitely two books you must reach out and buy."

—**Sue Scheff**, Parent Advocate, Internet Safety Expert and author of *Shame Nation: Preventing, Surviving & Overcoming Digital Shame*.

"The *8 Keys to End Bullying* activity book and companion guide offer much needed clarity on challenges related to bullying. This program equips caring adults and children with practical skills that work. The guides are full of true-to-life scenarios and creative, engaging activities. Adults and children who dive into the activities will be prepared with new ways of thinking about and responding to bullying to create positive change."

—**James Freeman, MA, CYC-P**, Training Director, Casa Pacifica Centers for Children and Families

"My 9-year-old daughter has had the unique opportunity of Signe Whitson being her school's guidance counselor the past few years. With Signe, she learned how to work through her feelings in a constructive and safe way after feeling bullied by a classmate. *The 8 Keys to End Bullying Activity Book* reinforces the invaluable skills and strategies Signe has imparted to my daughter at school. Other children and parents who want help coping with and understanding bullying behaviors will benefit greatly from this book."

—**Tara Schwartz**, mother of a 9-year-old, Pennsylvania

Also by Signe Whitson

The 8 Keys to End Bullying Activity Book for Kids & Tweens

8 Keys to End Bullying: Strategies for Parents & Schools

8 Keys to Mental Health Series
Babette Rothschild, Series Editor

The 8 Keys series of books, edited by Babette Rothschild, provides readers with brief, inexpensive, and high-quality self-help books on a variety of topics in mental health. Each volume is written by an expert in the field, someone who is capable of presenting evidence-based information in a concise and clear way. These books stand out by offering cutting-edge, relevant theory in easily digestible portions, written in an accessible style. The tone is respectful of the reader and the messages are immediately applicable. Filled with exercises and practical strategies, these books empower readers to help themselves.

THE 8 KEYS TO END BULLYING
ACTIVITY BOOK COMPANION GUIDE
FOR PARENTS & EDUCATORS

Signe Whitson

W.W. Norton & Company
Independent Publishers Since 1923
New York • London

For information about permission to reproduce selections from this book, write to Permissions, W. W. Norton & Company, Inc., 500 Fifth Avenue, New York, NY 10110

For information about special discounts for bulk purchases, please contact W. W. Norton Special Sales at specialsales@wwnorton.com or 800-233-4830

Manufacturing by LSC Crawfordsville
Book design by Vicki Fischman
Production manager: Christine Critelli

Library of Congress Cataloging-in-Publication Data
ISBN: 978-0-393-71182-0 (pbk.)

W. W. Norton & Company, Inc., 500 Fifth Avenue, New York, N.Y. 10110
www.wwnorton.com

W. W. Norton & Company Ltd., 15 Carlisle Street, London W1D, 3BS

1 2 3 4 5 6 7 8 9 0

To Richard, Hannah, and Elise

and to young people everywhere
who stand up, speak out, help others,
and choose kindness always.

Contents

KEY 5: LEVEL-UP YOUR SKILLS TO HANDLE BULLYING   131

KEY 6: BE KNOWN FOR BEING KIND   185

Acknowledgments

As I say to my students and note often in this Companion Guide, *words matter*. And so it is only fitting for me to acknowledge with words my love, gratitude, and admiration for the many people whose actions, experiences, stories, suggestions, wisdom and encouragement inspired me to write the *8 Keys to End Bullying* books, especially:

My daughters, Hannah and Elle, who are the most interesting people I know and whose empathy and kindness make me proud every single day. May your voices always be strong, confident, and kind and may your lives be blessed with love, laughter, hard work, and the knowledge that you make the world a better place. Thank you for being you—I love you more than mere *words* could ever say.

My husband, Richard, who has always been so encouraging of my writing and so understanding when I give him that look that says, "Shhhhhhh! I'm writing. I'll see you in a few hours." I love you and appreciate you.

My mom, Karen, who is the first real-live author I ever knew and my forever role-model of kindness, generosity, and unconditional love.

Ben Yarling at W.W. Norton, who was a champion of this Activity Book & Companion Guide from the very beginning. Your vision for what these books could be and creative suggestions all along the way were tremendously helpful. I am very grateful for your ideas and input and humbled by your belief in me. Thank you.

My students at Circle of Seasons Charter School: you have been some of my greatest teachers. What an honor it is to be your School Counselor (your Queen Signe) and to be part of your young lives. I love watching you grow and am proud of each and every one of you. Thank you for being among the first 'recipients' of many of the activities included in this Activity Book and for showing me first-hand how to make the lessons as helpful as possible to students everywhere.

Phil Arnold, the COS Board, and our amazingly supportive faculty: thank you for allowing me the time away from school that I needed to work on these books. I know that you took on extra roles in order to support our kiddos when I was not in the building and I appreciate all that you do, every day.

Nicholas Long, Frank Fecser, and my LSCI Institute colleagues around the globe: thank you for teaching me so early on in my career to always look beyond behavior and make time to genuinely understand the experiences, thoughts, and feelings that underlie the actions of young people. This framework guides all of my best work with kids. What's more, this fundamental belief in the power of relationships has led me to always persist in reaching out to kids who seem unreachable and to insist that kids who bully are worthy of more than just rote punishments and alienating labels.

Mary Kate Joseph, Kiely Ostfeld, and Kelly Richenaker: You are outstanding examples of what it takes to create cultures of kindness in classrooms. When I write about teachers who bring an end to bullying by prioritizing strong, positive connections with students, I am writing about you. When I describe professionals who infuse problem-solving, empathy-building, and social skills development into every subject they teach, I am describing you. And when I gratefully think of the difference-makers in my own daughters' lives, I am thinking of you! You are true champions of children and I am beyond lucky to know you and learn from you.

A Note to Companion Guide Readers

Dear Parents & Professionals:

Conflict happens. Friendship struggles and occasional abuses of social power by kids, tweens, and teens are as inevitable as acne, hormones, and heartbreaks. While most of us have probably wished at some point or another that we could put our young loved ones into a bubble and protect them from the pain associated with peer relationships, the truth is we cannot—and in reality should not—do so.

Every helpful adult understands that conflict can be a learning opportunity for a young person and that our role is to help the children we care for become competent in handling conflict independently and with dignity. The 8 *Keys to End Bullying Activity Book for Kids & Tweens* offers more than 40 activities, experiments, quizzes, and games to help your child(ren) develop specific skills to do just that, including effective strategies for standing up for themselves, reaching out to victims of cruelty, stopping cyberbullying, connecting to trustworthy adults, choosing healthy friendships, showing empathy for peers, and much, much more.

Sadly, some conflicts among young people go far beyond rudeness in the lunch line or mean behavior among friends. When bullying happens, we are no longer talking about "kids will be kids" stuff, but rather we are dealing with purposeful, patterned aggression that creates a level of powerlessness in a young person that he or she cannot reverse on their own. While parents and professionals often struggle with the question "To intervene or not to intervene?" the bottom line is this: Young people need skills for handling bullying and they need an adult's support and guidance to handle it well.

This *Companion Guide* to the *8 Keys to End Bullying Activity Book for Kids & Tweens* offers important insights, guidance, and strategies for empowering young people to understand and manage conflict well when they can and to reach out for help when it is needed. The fun, engaging learning opportunities provided in the Kids' *Activity Book* open the door for young people to talk with you about bullying and other friendship struggles and to learn enduring skills for healthy conflict management.

A KEY-BY-KEY GUIDE TO THE ACTIVITIES

The *Activity Book for Kids & Tweens* puts key concepts from the original *8 Keys to End Bullying: Strategies for Parents & Schools* text into action. Using a workbook format, it provides hands-on learning opportunities and skills practice for young people to reflect the *8 Keys* content areas listed below. (Please note that some Key titles have been changed in the kids' *Activity Book* to offer more youth-friendly, relatable wording. In the Guide below, I offer both titles for your ease of reference.)

KEY 1: Know Bullying When You See Bullying

Activity Book title: KNOW THE BASICS OF BULLYING

The five activities in this section bring Key 1 concepts to life by showing kids how to recognize bullying in all of its diverse forms and how to distinguish toxic bullying from less dangerous forms of aggression such as rudeness and mean behavior. Young people are empowered as they learn that they have *choices* for how to handle any type of bullying that occurs in their life.

KEY 2: Establish Connections With Kids

Activity Book title: CONNECT WITH PEOPLE YOU TRUST

In this section, four activities are provided to apply Key 2 concepts. Young readers gain skills for establishing meaningful connections with others, including seeking out trusting relationships with helping adults and forming healthy friendships with positive peers. Kids learn key differences between *tattling* and *telling* and are empowered to connect with trustworthy adults though the creation of an individualized Safety Plan.

KEY 3: Stop Bullying Whenever You See Bullying

Activity Book title: STOP BULLYING WHENEVER YOU SEE IT

The four activities in Key 3 offer young readers the opportunity to learn about and practice specific skills for assertive communication. Kids learn about "cotton" and "sandpaper" words and practice using *Mean, Meek,* and *Mean-It* voices to respond to conflict and bullying. This new knowledge and experience gives kids the confidence to intervene effectively and to stop bullying whenever they see it.

KEY 4: Deal Directly With Cyberbullying

Activity Book title: BE CYBERBULLYING FREE

The seven activities in this section put Key 4 concepts into action by teaching readers specific rules, strategies, and skills for using technology safely and respectfully. Key 4 activities acknowledge the pervasive presence of technology in kids' lives and celebrate the fun ways that gadgets connect kids with peers while empowering them to use their devices wisely.

KEY 5: Build Social and Emotional Competence

Activity Book title: LEVEL-UP YOUR SKILLS TO HANDLE BULLYING

Giving kids skills to manage bullying independently and with dignity is the essence of building social and emotional competence. This section offers eight activities that apply Key 5 concepts, as readers learn specific skills for regulating emotional responses to bullying, showing empathy, and resolving friendship problems. At a level that is both fascinating and understandable, elementary and middle school readers alike learn how various parts of their brain are activated during bullying and how to use the thinking, logical part of their brain to choose effective responses to challenging situations.

KEY 6: Turn Bystanders Into Buddies

Activity Book title: BE KNOWN FOR BEING KIND

This section offers four activities that bring Key 6 concepts to life by teaching kids specific skills to intervene on behalf of a victim before, during, and after an incident of bullying. Each activity is designed to help readers realize that reaching out to others is easier than they think and that they play a very powerful role in bringing an end to bullying.

KEY 7: Reach Out to Kids Who Bully

Activity Book title: REACH OUT TO KIDS WHO BULLY (No change!)

The paradox of bullying is that kids who push people away through their cruel behaviors, exclusionary activities, and unapologetic intimidation are often kids who need others the most. The five activities in this section reinforce Key 7 concepts by teaching readers specific skills such as empathy for the experiences of others, the ripple effect of their behavior, and pride in the strengths they bring to their class, their school, their family, and their community.

KEY 8: Keep the Conversation Going

Activity Book title: KEEP TALKING ABOUT ENDING BULLYING

This section offers three activities to put Key 8 concepts into action by encouraging young people to consider the practical, day-to-day, powerful ways that they can create awareness about the problem of bullying and initiate grassroots, solution-focused campaigns to bring an end to unwanted aggression in all of its forms.

HOW TO USE THE COMPANION GUIDE

The *Companion Guide* is designed to be used in conjunction with the *8 Keys to End Bullying Activity Book for Kids & Tweens*. While many of the pages in the *Activity Book* can be completed independently by upper elementary and middle school students, each lesson will be enhanced by the use of the follow-up questions, extra information, writing prompts, and bonus activities found only in the *Companion Guide*.

For each *Companion Guide* Activity, you will find:

- A brief introduction that previews the purpose of the lesson and skills kids will learn
- A "What Kids Learn" section that provides you with the complete text of the lesson from the *Activity Book*
- A "What Adults Need to Know" section that offers background information, research findings, and additional insights not included in the *Activity Book*
- A "Tips to Helps Kids Understand the Activity" section that is filled with discussion prompts and thought-provoking questions that challenge kids to take their learning to the next level. Each "tip" is designed to support and enhance the activity in a way that could not be accomplished by kids working entirely on their own.

The *Companion Guide* is meant to be versatile. Whether you are a parent working one on one with your own child or a schoolteacher, therapist, counselor, or youth leader working with groups of kids, each lesson can be easily customized to accommodate your needs. Likewise, some kids will use their *Activity Book* independently and at their own pace, turning to adults only to process specific ideas or practice new skills, while others will complete the activities as part of a small group or class, relying on adults to assign each activity and lead each discussion. As long as kids are engaged by the *Activity Book*, there is no wrong way to use it!

TALKING TO KIDS ABOUT BULLYING

It's not always easy for kids to talk to adults about friendships problems. Overwhelming feelings of embarrassment and humiliation prevent many young people from revealing their struggles with bullying; fear of being labeled a "tattletale" or "crybaby" holds still more kids back from open and honest conversations with parents, teachers, coaches, and other trusted adults. Each activity in the *Activity Book* is designed to speak directly to individuals through relatable language and universal examples while keeping topics global enough to show young readers in a non-threatening way that they are not alone in experiencing unwanted cruelty at the hands of their peers. What's more, the fun, engaging nature of each activity in the *Activity Book* makes it enjoyable—and therefore easier—for young people to talk candidly about friendship challenges.

Connecting with Young People Who Bully Others:

While many kids who have been bullied find it difficult to talk about their experiences, it is just as true that many adults find it challenging to talk to kids who bully their peers. As parents and professionals, we often have an emotional response to reports of cruelty; our first instinct is to reach out to protect victims, and our second is to swiftly punish aggressors. The truth, however, is that *every child has a story*, and while sometimes bullying situations are very black and white, with an innocent and a guilty party easily identifiable, more often there are layers and layers of information that need to be culled before absolute verdicts can be handed down. When talking to kids about bullying, it is critical that adults look beyond the most obvious level of behavior and aim to understand the background information, thoughts, and feelings of all the children involved. Some questions that are universally helpful for gathering information and reaching out to kids who bully include:

- *Tell me about what happened on the bus (in class/at lunch/etc.).*
  - ◊ This gives young people the opportunity to tell the story from their perspective. Will some kids lie or cover up their cruel behaviors? Of course. Is it still worthwhile to give each child the experience of feeling heard and understood? Absolutely. The information you can gather by offering each child the chance to be listened to is invaluable.

◊ What's more, the relationship you work to build with all children—even those presumed guilty—is the critical element in creating a genuine connection. Without strong adult connections, kids who bully act without the hindrance of disapproval by a grown-up that matters to them (Whitson, 2014), which puts us all in a very vulnerable position.

- *How do you and _____ usually get along? Has this ever happened before?*
  - ◊ It is helpful to establish whether there is a pattern of hostility and cruel behavior or whether you are dealing with an isolated incident.
- *Who else was there when this happened?*
  - ◊ Kids who bully are often seeking peer attention, peer approval, and the boost in social power they receive by dominating peer interactions. Gathering information about who else was involved is often a critical element of the story.
- *What were you trying to do? What did you hope would happen?*
  - ◊ Asking questions to understand a child's intentions is extremely helpful. Sometimes a child's only motivation is to get back at someone, to teach them a lesson, or to establish a higher rank on the school's social ladder. Other times, kids act out impulsively, temporarily lose their cool, aim to defend themselves, or act on behalf of someone else. This behavior looks like bullying when, in reality, there is much more to the story than initially meets the eye.
- *How would you feel if someone said that/did that to you?*
  - ◊ Questions aimed at increasing empathy can be helpful in bullying situations. Asking about a young person's emotional regard for others is also an important way of determining if the young person seems to lack empathy.

These five questions are just a start—a way of beginning a dialogue with a young person who bullies so as to begin the process of helping them change. Remember: Young people, by their very nature, are works in progress. When they behave badly—as most of them will do from time to time—our job is to not to brand them as bullies, troublemakers, or bad kids, but rather to reach out to them and teach them better ways to behave. This sort of empathic response is, after all, exactly what we want to instill in all of our young people. More ideas for how to talk to kids who bully are provided in Key 7 of both the original *8 Keys to End Bullying* book and this *Companion Guide.*

One final suggestion: Whenever possible (read: *always*) allow young people to take the lead in conversations on the topic of bullying. Open-ended questions such as the ones suggested in this *Companion Guide* are ideal for breaking the ice and encouraging children to let down their guard when it comes to talking about emotionally charged subject matter. On the other hand, the sense of being interrogated by question after question from adults—however well-intentioned—is one of the surest, fastest, and most permanent ways to shut down a child's desire to talk. Please always keep in mind that the prompts in the *Companion Guide* are meant to start conversations; ideally, the young person will do much of the rest. After all, it's no coincidence that the letters in the word "listen" can be rearranged to spell the word "silent."

I always love to hear from those of you living and working directly with kiddos. Please email me your feedback on any of the activities, games, quizzes, or material in the *Activity Book* and *Companion Guide* to signe@ signewhitson.com. You can also reach me and find the most up-to-date information through my website, www.signewhitson.com.

Have fun, be strong, and choose kindness always!

Signe Whitson

Know the Basics of Bullying

ACTIVITY 1 What Is Bullying?

On just about any given day in any given school, you can hear a teacher warn a student against bullying or hear a young person accuse a peer of being a bully. It's a great thing that adults and kids are united in stopping cruelty. On the other hand, there may be days when you—and the youngsters in your life—get so tired of hearing the word "bully" tossed around that you stop taking the word seriously.

But *not* paying attention to bullying is dangerous for everyone! That's why the first priority of the *8 Keys to End Bullying Activity Book for Kids & Tweens* is to establish a clear and consistent definition of the word "bullying" and give kids the knowledge to tell the difference between this serious—and potentially dangerous—behavior and less harmful (though still painful!) things like rudeness and mean behavior.

WHAT KIDS LEARN

In the *Activity Book for Kids and Tweens*, the following definitions and examples of rude, mean, and bullying behavior, first described by bestselling children's author, Trudy Ludwig (2013), are provided:

Rude = Accidentally saying or doing something hurtful.

Rude behaviors include:

- Burping out loud
- Butting in line
- Bragging about making a team
- Stepping on someone's foot by accident

Rude behaviors are usually thoughtless and ill-mannered, but they are not meant to hurt anyone.

Mean = Saying or doing something to hurt a person on purpose, once or maybe twice.

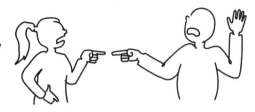

The main difference between "rude" and "mean" behavior is that rudeness is not usually planned. Mean behavior, on the other hand, is done on purpose.

Mean behaviors include:

- Making fun of what someone looks like or what they are wearing
  - Saying, "I don't like your short hair. You look like a boy."
  - Saying, "Gross. Why did you wear that dress?"
- Insulting someone's intelligence or ability
  - Saying, "You're so stupid."
  - Saying, "You stink at soccer."
- Saying or doing something unkind after a fight with a friend
  - Saying, "I hate you."
  - Taking something that doesn't belong to you.

Make no mistake: Mean behaviors are very hurtful and should be avoided at all times! Still, being mean is different from bullying. We'll talk about that next.

Kids who bully say or do something hurtful to others on purpose. They keep doing it again and again with no sense of guilt or shame. Kids who bully have more power than the kids they pick on. This power may come from being older, stronger, or bigger. It may also come from getting several kids to gang up on one target so that the target feels hurt and alone.

Bullying = Cruel behavior, done on purpose and repeated over time, that involves an imbalance of power.

KEY POINT

To understand bullying, remember the 3 P's:

1. It is done on **P**urpose. There is nothing "accidental" or unplanned about bullying.
2. It is a **P**attern. The cruelty happens over and over again.
3. It is all about **P**ower. The cruel person has more control and influence than the target.

For each type of behavior, *Activity Book* users are challenged to describe typical examples of the behaviors they see among their peers.

Why Do I Need to Know the Difference Between Being Rude, Being Mean, and Bullying?

It is important to know the difference between rude, mean, and bullying behavior so that you understand what you are dealing with and know how to respond. The skills in this Activity Book will help you know **what to say** and **what to do** anytime you see bullying. You will gain the *confidence* and *power* you need to help bring an end to bullying.

In the next Activity, you will read about situations that happened to young people in real life. You will then figure out if they are acts of rudeness, meanness, or bullying.

WHAT ADULTS NEED TO KNOW

The good news about our culture of round-the-clock news cycles and end-less social media status updates is that constant coverage and connectedness give adults more opportunity to bring attention to important issues. In the last few years, we have collectively paid attention to the issue of bullying like never before. Millions of school children have been given a voice, all 50 states in the U.S. have passed anti-bullying legislation, and scores of educators have been trained in important strategies to keep kids safe and dignified in schools and communities. These are significant achievements.

The bad news, however, is that gratuitous references to bullying have bred cynicism in some and spawned a bit of a "little boy who cried wolf" phenomenon in others. When people improperly classify rudeness and mean behavior as bullying, we are all put at risk of becoming numb to the true seriousness of the term and tuning out when truly troubled kids need adult intervention.

It is important to distinguish between rude, mean, and bullying behaviors so that parents, teachers, school administrators, counselors, police, youth workers, and kids all know what to pay attention to and when to intervene. To these ends, a Screening Tool for Reported Bullying Behavior is provided on page 8–9. This tool may be used by professionals or parents in schools, youth organizations, small groups, homes, or any setting in which allegations of bullying occur regularly and responsible adults need to discern between levels of aggression in order to respond appropriately. As the Screening Tool directions indicate, affirmative responses to the four questions give a strong indication that *bullying behavior has occurred* and needs to be more thoroughly investigated by a designated authority. Negative responses, on the other hand, indicate that a problematic behavior that *has not risen to the level of bullying* has likely occurred. These behaviors are likely best addressed by the adult who receives the report from the child, according to school, group, or family rules. For use in schools and youth-oriented groups, the Screening Tool also provides space for adults to briefly document and describe the reported behavior.

TIPS TO HELP KIDS UNDERSTAND THE ACTIVITY:

- Talk to kids about rude, mean, and bullying behavior, using the definitions and terms provided in the Activity. Check to make sure the young person(s) genuinely understands the distinct characteristics of each one.
- Encourage dialogue about the typical ways that kids see rude, mean, and bullying behavior in their schools and communities. Assure young people that your goal is not to "take names" or "get anyone in trouble," but rather to convey your genuine interest in learning about the types of behaviors kids are experiencing among their peers.
- Encourage discussion about how most behaviors occur on a continuum and explore how rudeness can become meanness, which can become bullying over time.
- Ask kids for their thoughts on why it's important to make a distinction between rude, mean, and bullying behaviors.
- Encourage kids to talk about occasions in which they mistook a mean comment for bullying or excused actual bullying as simple rudeness.
- If you are working with kids in a school or community setting, assign small groups of kids (three to five kids per group) to develop three written scenarios—one that represents rudeness, one that represents meanness, and one that represents bullying.
  - ◊ Challenge group members to carefully think through how each scenario differs from the others.
  - ◊ If time allows, it can be most impactful to encourage kids to act out their scenarios as mini-skits for the large group.
  - ◊ Facilitate discussion after each skit about what behaviors were demonstrated and why they are characteristic of rudeness, meanness, or bullying.

Screening Tool for Reported Bullying Behavior

1. Was the behavior carried out on purpose?

      Yes   No

2. Was the behavior intended to cause harm? (Harm may be physical, verbal, relational, social, emotional, and/or via electronic communications)

      Yes   No

3. Have there been repetitive and patterned acts of this behavior? (Repeated aggression is defined as an average of two or more incidents per week, over the course of two or more weeks.)

      Yes   No

    3a. Does the behavior include electronic communications that can be viewed an unlimited number of times by an unlimited number of people?

          Yes   No

4. Does an imbalance of power exist and/or is the target of the behavior unable to stop the bullying behavior from continuing?

      Yes   No

YES answers to Questions 1, 2, 3, <u>and</u> 4, give a strong indication that *bullying behavior has occurred* and that this incident should be more thoroughly investigated. Please forward this completed form to a designated authority within 24 hours. Please include a brief summary of the incident on the following page.

A **NO** answer to <u>any</u> of the Questions above (not including 3a), indicates that a problem behavior that *does not rise to the level of bullying* has likely occurred. The incident should be addressed with the young person(s) in accordance with school, group, or family rules. Every effort should be taken to address the behavior as soon as possible.

Screening Tool for Reported Bullying Behavior

Student Name: Date:

Grade: Teacher: Time of Incident:

Name of Person Completing Report:

Incident Summary:

_____
Signature of Person Completing Report

© Whitson 2016

ACTIVITY 2 Is It Rude, Is It Mean, or Is It Bullying?

In this activity, young people get the opportunity to put their new knowledge of the important distinctions between rude, mean, and bullying behaviors to use as they read 10 real-life scenarios and are challenged to properly identify each one. Below, you will find the 10 scenarios from the *Activity Book*, followed by a detailed explanation of how to classify each one. (An Answer Key and rationale are also provided in the *Activity Book*, although they are on a separate page from the 10 scenarios.) This *Companion Guide* includes three brand-new scenarios—not provided in the *Activity Book*—for additional discussion.

WHAT KIDS LEARN

Directions:

For each of the situations below, decide if the behavior is rude, mean, or bullying. Circle the BEST response. (*Correct answers are found on the last page of the Activity.*)

EXAMPLE:

Kayla tells MacKenzie that she can't sit with her on the bus today. Kayla says she is saving the seat for someone else.

 Rude   Mean   Bullying

COMPANION GUIDE EXPLANATION: Kayla is being **rude**, but there is no evidence of intentional meanness, repetitive behavior, or a power imbalance.

1. Lucas is in a bad mood. He tells Damien that he is the worst player in the whole grade. He says Damien can't play soccer at recess.

Rude   Mean   Bullying

COMPANION GUIDE EXPLANATION: Lucas is being **mean**. It appears that his words are intended to hurt Damien. There is no evidence of a pattern of cruel behavior or a power imbalance, however.

---

2. Katie always bosses Talia around. On Friday, Talia makes plans to go to the school dance with her new friend, Gwen. Katie tells Talia that if she hangs out at the dance with Gwen, everyone will think she is a total weirdo and no one will like her anymore. At lunch, Katie tells everyone that it would be a really funny joke to all laugh out loud when Talia gets there.

Rude   Mean   Bullying

COMPANION GUIDE EXPLANATION: Katie is acting like a **bully**. She has created an unfair balance of power by getting all the girls at the lunch table to laugh at Talia. She is also using words like "everyone" and "no one" to threaten Talia about how she will be left out if she does not do what Katie wants her to do.

---

3. Kevin and David are close friends. In school, they have a fight. Kevin calls David a name and David shoves him.

Rude   Mean   Bullying

COMPANION GUIDE EXPLANATION: Kevin and David are engaging in rough play (Olweus, 2007), or **rude** behavior. This is not bullying because the boys are usually friends, the power balance is relatively equal, and the boys are not intending to harm each other.

4. Maggie keeps making fun of Jessie for hanging out with boys and wearing long basketball shorts to school every day. In gym, Maggie tells Jessie to play on the boys' team. In math, she writes the words "You're so gay" on Jessie's desk.

Rude   Mean   Bullying

COMPANION GUIDE EXPLANATION: Maggie is acting like a **bully**. She is making fun of Jessie repeatedly and trying to hurt her feelings. It is never okay to call people names based on how they dress or what they look like. The word "gay" should never, ever be used as a put-down

5. Madelyn won't talk to Ella. When Ella asks her what is wrong, Madelyn says, "Figure it out!" She gives Ella dirty looks when they pass each other in the hall. Ella tries to find out from Madelyn's friends what the problem is. They will not talk to Ella. For 2 weeks, Ella is left out at lunch and blocked from group texts.

Rude   Mean   Bullying

COMPANION GUIDE EXPLANATION: Madelyn is acting like a **bully**. She is using the withdrawal of her friendship as a weapon to hurt Ella. What's more, she is getting her friends involved, which creates a power imbalance and leaves Ella feeling isolated and alone. What would be most helpful in this situation would be for Madelyn to talk to Ella directly about the reason she is upset and for the other girls to refuse to exclude Ella from their social group.

6. Brady tells JP he will beat him up if he touches his cars. He then shoves JP out of his way. During math, he throws a spitball at JP. He also kicks JP's chair out from under him. He tells JP he will punch him in the face if JP tells the teacher.

Rude   Mean   Bullying

COMPANION GUIDE EXPLANATION: Brady is acting like a **bully**. He is engaging in repetitive cruel behavior designed to hurt JP. He is using intimidation and threats to create a power imbalance.

7. Olivia thinks that Lily and Ariana are becoming close friends. She worries that she will be left out. She is nice to Ariana at school, but she is always insulting her online. Last night, she texted a rumor about Ariana to the whole class.

Rude   Mean   Bullying

COMPANION GUIDE EXPLANATION: Olivia feels as if she is losing some of her social power as she watches Lily and Ariana form a close friendship. Instead of working to strengthen her connection with both girls, she is attempting to gain power over Ariana by targeting her online through cruel tweets and embarrassing posts. Olivia is misusing social power and acting like a **bully**

8. Maeve and Kristy are playing a game. Tasha walks over to them. Maeve and Kristy look up briefly and smile. Then they go right back to their game. Tasha feels left out. She yells at the other girls for ignoring her.

Rude   Mean   Bullying

COMPANION GUIDE EXPLANATION: Maeve and Kristy were involved in a game before Tasha was present. When Tasha arrived, they smiled at her briefly but did not stop their game to talk with her or include her in their play. Maeve and Kristy showed a level of **rude** behavior by not more fully acknowledging Tasha. However, there is no evidence that this was planned ignoring or meant to hurt Tasha's feelings.

Tasha's loud reaction to Maeve and Kristy likely attracted attention to their behavior and escalated the situation to a bigger problem than it needed to be. Tasha would have been better off staying calm and letting the girls know that she wanted to hang out with them when their game was over.

9. Kaitlyn and Gabby are best friends. In school, they have a fight. Gabby calls Kaitlyn a name, and Kaitlyn deletes Gabby from an online "friends" list. The next day, they make up and are friends again.

Rude   Mean   Bullying

COMPANION GUIDE EXPLANATION: In the course of almost every friendship, there are bumps in the road. Even BFFs do not agree 100% of the time, and a real, healthy friendship is one that can withstand arguments and anger from time to time. Because we know that Kaitlyn and Gabby made up quickly, we can consider this an example of **mean** behavior.

Episodes of mean behavior can turn into drama between girls when their friends get involved, take sides, start gossip, and escalate the everyday argument into a hurtful war of words. *Whenever possible, it is better to keep a cool head and not add fuel to someone else's fight.* Also, be sure to discourage others from making a bad situation worse.

WHAT ADULTS NEED TO KNOW:

Now that we've dedicated the first two Activities of this book to talking about the important distinctions between rude, mean, and bullying behavior, it may surprise you to read these words of caution:

Young people will often come to you with very intense emotions over situations that you may now be able to clearly diagnose as only rude or mean. Having heard dire warnings about bullying from their parents, in school, and via television and online, kids are apt to overgeneralize and catastrophize all matters of conflict in three simple words: "I'm being bullied!"

While it is our job to help kids discern between levels of toxicity in behavior, it is just as important that as caring adults, we validate a child's feelings—no matter what. So, when a seven-year-old comes to you sobbing and accusing her best friend of being a bully because she sat with someone else on the bus ride home that afternoon, or your 12-year-old is seething and ready to take revenge on the "bullies" who picked him last for kickball in gym that particular day, skillfully apply your new knowledge of the 3 P's of bullying and fight the urge to insist, "Don't be upset," or, "That's not even bullying, silly!"

Rather, in the moment, it is most helpful to reach out to the young person, validate feelings through a statement such as, "I can tell you are really upset about this right now!" and assist them in calming down. It is critical for adults to understand that only *after* the young person trusts that you understand his feelings and is relaxed enough to talk about them (rather than cry, yell, accuse, etc.) can he begin to engage in a conversation about whether or not the upsetting behavior was actually bullying.

TIPS TO HELP KIDS UNDERSTAND THE ACTIVITY

Below, you will find three scenarios similar to the ones presented in the *Activity Book for Kids & Tweens*. These scenarios have not been seen by young readers yet, however. You can use them, along with the suggested answers and explanation, to further engage kids in a discussion about how (and why!) to know the difference between rude, mean, and bullying behavior.

SCENARIO 1

Kiely and Kaitlyn have been neighbors and best friends since first grade. In fourth grade, Wendy moves into their neighborhood. At first, Kiely and Kaitlyn are nice to Wendy, but they soon agree that Wendy is "sorta weird" and "such a crybaby." Kiely and Kaitlyn begin to think it's funny to say little things that predictably trigger big emotional reactions from Wendy—and then to laugh it off by saying, "We were just joking. Geesh. We didn't know you would be so sensitive."

ANSWER: Kiely and Kaitlyn are acting like **bullies**. As girls who have had a tight bond for four years already, they have a social power advantage over Wendy—the new girl who just moved to the neighborhood and is relatively isolated socially. They are fooling themselves into believing that it's "funny" to intentionally say things that they know will hurt Wendy and cause her to act out emotionally. Doing it over and over again, and hiding behind the rationalization of "We were just joking," is a common method of relational bullying. Adults are helpful when they help put a swift end to this type of behavior and refuse to let Kiely and Kaitlyn justify their bullying behavior or continue to manipulate Wendy.

SCENARIO 2

Chris posted a photo of himself and his friend Amber on social media. Since it was a really good picture of him, he didn't take into account how embarrassed Amber might be by how bad the photo was of her. By the time she saw it online, it seemed as if their whole grade had seen it too—and had posted all kind of unflattering comments about her appearance. Chris took the photo down as soon as he realized his mistake.

ANSWER: Chris's decision to post the photo without Amber's permission was both **rude** and thoughtless, although there is no indication from this scenario that he did it intentionally to hurt or embarrass her. Rather, he thought he looked good in the photo and failed to consider Amber's privacy or her feelings. The fact that Chris took it down right away affirms that his intentions were good, even if his impulsive judgment was poor.

SCENARIO 3

Tessa thinks of herself as the best dresser in her grade. When Molly comes into school one day wearing new jeans and boots, all of the girls ooh and ah about her outfit. Tessa feels jealous of the attention Molly is getting. On the way to school cafeteria later that morning, Tessa walks up to Molly and quietly smirks, "Aren't those the jeans from the clearance section at Bargain Hut, Molly? Were they out of the ones in your actual size? Those look a little tight to me!"

ANSWER: Tessa's comments to Molly are **mean**. Her jealousy over the fashion attention Molly is receiving seems to have motivated her hurtful comments. As far as we know, however, there is no history of Tessa insulting Molly, and since Tessa is the only one who seems to be behaving unkindly, there is no obvious power imbalance.

ACTIVITY 3 What Does Bullying Look Like?

In the first two Activities of this workbook, we defined bullying as having three key elements: Purpose, Pattern, and Power. In this Activity, kids learn the four most common types of bullying and list three to five specific ways that they see each type occurring in their school and community.

WHAT KIDS LEARN

Bullying may be physical, verbal, relational, or carried out via technology:

Physical bullying: This kind of bullying includes a range of aggressive behaviors in which one person aims to cause bodily harm to another person.

Verbal bullying: Some people say that "words will never hurt you," but anyone who has been on the receiving end of verbal bullying knows that cruel words and scary threats can indeed be very painful.

Relational bullying: In relational bullying, kids use friendship--and the threat of taking their friendship away—to hurt others. This is the type of bullying most often referred to as "drama." Because it often happens within the context of a once-trusting friendship, drama can be especially confusing and hurtful.

Cyberbullying: This is a specific form of bullying that involves technology. As you will see in later Activities in this book, cyberbullying can be especially destructive because of how quickly and how widely cruel messages can spread.

In their Activity book, kids are provided with short-answer, checklist, and circling tasks to correctly describe and identify examples of each type of bullying. An Answer Key is provided so that young readers can review their responses.

WHAT ADULTS NEED TO KNOW

When young people become well versed in recognizing bullying behaviors quickly, they are better equipped to respond to the situation effectively. How are *your* skills in knowing bullying when you see it?

Key 1 of 8 *Keys to End Bullying: Strategies for Parents and Schools* provides comprehensive information on this topic as well as on related red flags of bullying, such as understanding which young people tend to bully their peers, why certain kids choose bullying behavior, where youth tend to act out their unwanted aggression (hint: it's in all the places and spaces where adults are typically not present!), who are the young people most vulnerable to being bullied by their peers, and what are the warning signs that a child has become a victim of bullying.

Before engaging kids in a discussion about the four types of bullying behavior, make a list of the ways in which you have seen bullying played out. Use the four categories (physical aggression, verbal aggression, relational aggression, and cyberbullying) to organize your list. Challenge yourself to write down at least five specific examples for each category. Truly, the list is almost endless.

Next, think about which behaviors on the list occur most commonly to the kids that you know. Put a star next to these behaviors. These high-frequency behaviors merit your extra attention and responsiveness. Moreover, these are the key behaviors that you can educate kids about, teaching them specific strategies for recognizing and responding effectively.

TIPS TO HELP KIDS UNDERSTAND THE ACTIVITY

- Encourage kids to talk about the specific behaviors they listed in each category.
  - ◊ Are there specific bullying behaviors on their list that occur most frequently?
  - ◊ Are there behaviors that occur less frequently but inflict more physical or emotional pain?
- Ask kids to identify which behaviors on their list they would be most likely to report to a trustworthy adult.
- Challenge young people to consider if there are certain bullying behaviors that cause more confusion or humiliation to young people and that therefore they would be less likely to report to adults.
- Explain to kids that from the vantage point of most adults, physical and verbal aggression are much easier to actually see happening than relational and online aggression. Encourage kids to think through how they can make helping adults aware of more subtle and hidden forms of bullying.
- Last, encourage kids to brainstorm specific actions they can take to effectively respond to the different types of behavior on their list. Write down their responses without offering extensive guidance or judgment. Let them know that you will revisit the list with them after upcoming activities. Assure kids that as they make their way through the *Activity Book*, they will learn all kinds of strategies and skills for responding effectively to bullying in all of its forms.

ACTIVITY 4 Four Types of Bullying

In Activity 3, young people learned about four types of bullying behavior (physical, verbal, relational and cyberbullying) and listed the ways they see each type of bullying play out in daily life. In Activity 4, kids are presented with a comprehensive list of common bullying behaviors and are asked to categorize them. Then, young people are challenged to journal about the type of bullying that impacts their life most often as well as the type that is most painful for them. Kids will write about a specific situation in which they experienced bullying and describe how they handled it at the time.

WHAT KIDS LEARN

Kids are presented with the following list of typical bullying behaviors and asked to circle the ones they have observed or been involved in. Then, on the following activity pages, they are asked to classify each behavior as typical of physical, verbal, or relational bullying or cyberbullying. As a *Companion Guide* reader, you are provided with an Answer Key as part of the checklist. Use the following guide to assist kids, as necessary, in checking their answers:

(**P**) = Physical bullying   (**R**) = Relational bullying
(**V**) = Verbal bullying   (**C**) = Cyberbullying

Typical Bullying Behaviors

Hitting (**P**)

Cursing (**V**)

Posting cruel comments online (**C**)

Giving the silent treatment (**R**)

Kicking (**P**)

Pushing (**P**)

Tripping (**P**)

Elbowing (**P**)

Posting party photos online to show who was NOT invited to the party (**C**)

Talking about plans in front of people who are not included (**R**)

Teasing (**V**)

Calling names (**V**)

Threatening (**V**)

Starting rumors online (**C**)

Setting up a fake social media account (**C**)

Spitting (**P**)

Talking behind someone's back (**V**)

Telling everyone to ignore someone (**R**)

Altering someone's profile photo in a cruel way (**C**)

Making fun of someone in a group chat (**C**)

Insulting (**V**)

Gossiping (**R**)

Leaving someone out at lunch on purpose (**R**)

Saying something cruel on purpose, then saying "Just joking" (**R**)

Not allowing someone to sit with the group on the bus (**R**)

WHAT ADULTS NEED TO KNOW

It is important for adults and kids to note that there will be some natural overlap in the four categories of bullying behavior. For example:

- "Posting party photos online to show who was NOT invited" is a tactic of both relational bullying and cyberbullying. Because it happens via technology, it is classified in the Answer Key as cyberbullying, although a young person would be perfectly correct in labeling it *relational bullying*.
- "Saying something cruel on purpose, then saying 'Just joking'" is an example of both verbal and relational aggression. For the purposes of this book, it has been labeled relational aggression, since kids often use rationalizations such as "Just kidding" to justify social exclusion. Cruel words—even when disguised as jokes—are just as accurately covered by the term *verbal bullying*.

The fact that bullying behaviors don't always fall neatly into single categories—and that most kids who bully use multiple tactics to inflict repetitive acts of unwanted aggression—is all great fodder for discussion with kids.

TIPS TO HELP KIDS UNDERSTAND THE ACTIVITY

- Encourage young people to talk about the items they circled in the checklist. Which are the behaviors they see most often at school?
  - ◊ Are there certain behaviors they are most likely to see outside the classroom?
  - ◊ At lunch?
  - ◊ On the school bus?
  - ◊ On a sports team?
  - ◊ With a youth group?

    ◊ At home?

    ◊ Online?

- Which type of bullying impacts their own life the most?
- What kind of bullying is easiest for them to know how to handle?
- Which type of bullying is most difficult for them to know how to respond to?
- Encourage kids to talk about a time when they have been on the receiving end of bullying. What happened? What kind(s) of bullying took place?
- As a lead-in to Activity 5, ask kids to talk about a time when they acted like a bully toward someone else. Let kids know that we all have bad days and behave in ways that we later regret; being able to acknowledge and take responsibility for these occasions gives us the opportunity to learn from mistakes and fix them so that they do not become a pattern.

ACTIVITY 5 What's Your Bully-Busting Spirit Animal?

In the first section of their *Activity Book*, kids are learning key concepts and terms related to conflict and bullying. The goal is to empower them to know bullying whenever they see it by developing awareness of the red flags of unwanted aggression. This final activity from Key 1 turns an important corner from conceptual understanding to practical skill-building, as kids learn the most effective ways to handle any type of bullying in their lives.

WHAT KIDS LEARN

To empower young people, a primary emphasis in their *Activity Book* is to teach them that they always have *choices* when it comes to how to respond to bullying. Using the "What's Your Bully-Busting Spirit Animal?" quiz (reprinted below), kids read about real-life situations and are asked to choose the response(s) that they think would be best to stop bullying behavior. At the end of the quiz, an Answer Key (also reprinted here) helps kids reflect on the likely consequences and outcomes of each choice while encouraging readers to choose the most effective strategies for stopping bullying.

- -

QUIZ TIME: What's Your Bully-Busting Spirit Animal?

What's Your Bully-Busting Spirit Animal?

1. Krystal and Shonnell sit together on the bus to school. Krystal is angry at Shonnell for being too noisy. She calls her "ugly" and says, "If you keep being so loud, I'm going to spit on you."

What do you think Shonnell should do?

A. Say, "If you spit on me, I'll punch you in the face."

B. Turn the other way and start talking to a nice kid in the next seat.

C. Think to herself, "I like the way I look. I'm going to keep my cool and not react to what Krystal just said."

D. Change the subject. Ask Krystal if she saw that funny episode of their favorite TV show last night.

E. Look Krystal in the eye. In a strong, steady voice, say, "That's gross. Don't say that."

2. Ricky likes to be in charge of everything in his neighborhood. When Preston gets to be team captain, Ricky gets mad. He picks up a dodgeball and throws it at Preston's head.

What do you think Preston should do?

A. Grab the ball and throw it at Ricky's face as hard as he can.

B. Look at his watch and tell the other kids that he has to be home for soccer practice. Then walk home to tell his parents what happened.

C. Count to 10 to give himself time to think about what to do.

D. Try to make the crowd laugh by falling to the ground and holding his head as if it were broken in 2 pieces.

E. Say, "That would've been a great shot—if the game had started yet, Ricky. Since it didn't, chill out."

3. Elizabeth tells Tina, "If you play with Jennie today, you can't be my friend." Tina ignores Elizabeth's threat and plays with Jennie during recess. At the end of the school day, Elizabeth tells 3 other girls that tomorrow is "Don't Talk to Tina Day." They all agree to ignore Tina in school all day long.

What do you think Tina should do?

A. Start a rumor about Elizabeth. Tell everyone that she has a crush on a classmate named Carlos and only changes her underwear once a week.

B. Spend time with other friends from the class. Act as if she isn't at all bothered by what Elizabeth and the other 3 girls are doing.

C. Remind herself that she is a great kid and a great friend. Remember that her mother always tells her to focus on friends that make her feel happy.

D. When she and Elizabeth are standing close together at their cubbies, say aloud, "It sure has been a quiet day. I really needed the quiet time today. Thanks!"

E. In a calm voice, say, "I guess you're mad that I played with Jennie and that's why you and the girls aren't talking to me today. I get it."

4. Jason takes a picture of Kenny in the locker room when he is changing for football practice. He posts it online without Kenny's permission. Most of the kids in their 5th-grade class see the picture of Kenny in his underwear.

What do you think Kenny should do?

A. Text all the girls in their grade an embarrassing photo of Jason pretending to kiss a Barbie doll.

B. Take a screen shot of the post. Show it to the school counselor and ask for her help.

C. Say to himself, "I know what to do in this situation. I can handle this problem."

D. Avoid going online for a few days until the situation is fixed.

E. Say to Jason, "That's so not cool. Delete the photo online and from your phone right now."

5. Morgan and Elsa are on the same soccer team. Elsa does not treat Morgan like a teammate. She points out Morgan's mistakes and laughs at her when she falls down. In one game, Morgan misses a shot on goal. Elsa groans loudly and shouts, "Again, Morgan? Have you scored at all this season? How did you even make the team, anyway?"

What do you think Morgan should do?

A. Next time she has the ball, kick it right at Elsa's head. Then, when the referee isn't watching, trip Elsa on purpose so that she falls flat on her face during the game.

B. Stay focused on the game at the moment. Talk to the coach after the game and get his help in handling Elsa's put-downs.

C. Remind herself that she is a great soccer player, a fantastic teammate, and someone who never gives up.

D. Take a deep breath. Think about where the other team's goalie will likely punt the ball. Encourage her teammates to pass to each other.

E. Say, "Knock it off, Elsa. We're a team, remember?"

Bully-Busting Quiz Choices

After completing the Quiz, kids are guided to reflect on their answers, using the following guide:

If you chose mostly A's, your Spirit Animal is the Tiger.

Your first thought in a conflict or bullying situation may be to attack. Like a tiger, you pounce on anyone who wrongs you. You feel strong and satisfied when you get revenge. The problem is that when you copy the behavior of someone who bullies, you make yourself look bad in the long run. When you meet violence with violence, bad things will continue to happen over and over again.

Instead of making your situation worse, consider the following better choices:

- Reach out to trustworthy friends and adults for protection
- Use positive messages to keep yourself strong
- Change the subject
- Walk away
- Use humor
- Stand up for yourself with strong words

You'll learn more about these helpful responses to bullying in the descriptions below and throughout your Activity Book!

If you chose mostly B's, your Spirit Animal is the Wolf.
Wolves are known as pack animals because they stick close together for protection and comfort. When bullying happens, you know that connecting with friends, family members, teachers, counselors, and other helping adults gives you the protection you need. Never be afraid to reach out to your pack and tell them what is going on in your life. Connecting with others is a sign of your smarts, your strength, and your courage!

If you chose mostly C's, your Spirit Animal is the Owl.
Like the owl, you are wise and have a strong mind. The positive messages that you repeat in your head (things like "I like the way I look" and "I can handle this") give you the confidence and power you need to cope with bullying. You are smart enough to choose your friends wisely and surround yourself with people that make you feel good about yourself.

If you chose mostly D's, your Spirit Animal is the Butterfly.
Just as the caterpillar changes into a butterfly, you are wise enough to know that in a bullying situation you can:

- change the subject of the conversation
- change the scene by walking away
- change a negative into a positive

- change your focus to the task at hand
- change the tone of the conversation from anger to humor
- change the tone of the conversation from anger to humor

If you chose mostly E's, your Spirit Animal is the Giraffe. I'll bet you're wondering what having a long neck has to do with handling bullying. Good question. Just as the tall giraffe doesn't need to stretch to reach the trees, you know that you do not need to stretch the truth. You are known for being honest and a straight shooter. You tell it like it is to anyone who bullies you. Like the giraffe, you speak the straight-up truth *without being hurtful* in the process. Keep on standing tall and speaking up for yourself in proud ways! You are a role model to those around you.

If you chose a mix of options, you have the Spirit of the Zookeeper.

You know many helpful ways to stop bullying. You are smart enough to choose the best one in any situation. Being flexible like that is great! It tells others that your confidence can't be shaken. You are strong enough to make great choices to stop all types of bullying. Just be sure to steer clear of hurtful or violent acts at all times, no matter how tempting they may be in the moment.

MORE TO THINK ABOUT

What Is Your Bully-Busting Spirit Animal?

WHAT DID THE QUIZ SAY YOUR SPIRIT ANIMAL IS?

_____

WHAT WOULD BE YOUR IDEAL SPIRIT ANIMAL?

_____

THINK ABOUT WAYS YOU MIGHT IMPROVE OR CHANGE YOUR BULLY-BUSTING STYLE. THEN DRAW A PICTURE OF YOUR CHOSEN BULLY-BUSTING SPIRIT ANIMAL BELOW:

(The Activity Book provides young readers with space to illustrate their spirit animal.)

WHAT ADULTS NEED TO KNOW

In the heat of a stressful moment, such as a bullying situation, kids often tense up and make choices based on emotions and instincts rather than on clear judgments and thought-out plans. (In Activity 21, kids will learn more about why their brain responds this way and what they can do about it.) Adults play a key role in preparing kids to respond well to bullying by talking about, planning for, and rehearsing effective coping strategies. The quiz scenarios provided in this Activity are a great springboard for discussion between you and a child or children on the various choices they can make when they encounter bullying, as well as the likely outcomes of each choice.

TIPS TO HELP KIDS UNDERSTAND THE ACTIVITY

- Encourage general conversation with kids about each identified response style—Tiger, Wolf, Owl, Butterfly, Giraffe, and Zookeeper. Compare and contrast each style.
- Share with kids the response style that you most typically use. If you have a real-life experience where your style was especially effective, consider sharing it as a learning moment for kids.
- Talk about the Tiger style with kids. Acknowledge that attack strategies are often very tempting, since they satisfy a child's short-term need for revenge. Encourage longer-term thinking, however, so that kids gain an understanding of the potentially dangerous consequences of meeting violence with violence.
- If a child shares with you that he or she feels physically threatened by a peer, always take the report seriously. As a helping adult, the way you set out to gather additional information and take real steps to ensure a child's well-being signals to young people that adults are trustworthy and that reaching out for help is an effective safety strategy. Specific strategies for "How to Respond

to a Child Who Talks About Bullying" are featured in Activity 6 of this *Companion Guide* and in Key 2 of 8 *Keys to End Bullying: Strategies for Parents & Schools.*

- Explore the Wolf style with kids. Ask them to explain in their own words why connecting with friends, teachers, school counselors, and family members (i.e., their "pack") is a helpful strategy for breaking bullying.
  - ◊ Emphasize that because of the power imbalance inherent in bullying dynamics, it is always important for kids who are bullied to reach out to others. Remind them that *connection can provide protection* (Whitson, 2011).
  - ◊ Let kids know that in the next Activity, they will be focusing on the important differences between tattling and telling—and finding out that reaching out to others during a bullying situation is never something to fear or be ashamed of.
- Encourage kids to think about how the wise Owl style of staying mentally strong and repeating positive self-talk can be effective in countering the impact of bullying. Challenge kids to generate positive self-statements that they can repeat to themselves whenever they encounter unwanted aggression.
- Ask kids why change, represented by the Butterfly, can be a helpful strategy for stopping bullying. In the quiz, readers consider situations where young people changed the subject, changed the tone of the conversation through humor, changed their environment by walking away, changed a negative into a positive, or changed their focus. Challenge readers to think about other types of changes that could be effective for breaking bullying.
- Acknowledge for kids that acting like a Giraffe can be one of the hardest styles to master. While it may seem as if being straight-up with your thoughts and feelings would be the easiest option, for most kids (and adults!), it is intimidating to confront others. Assertiveness—the skill of expressing emotions directly and without hurting others—is a style that kids can learn, however. In Activities 11, 12 and 13, readers will learn and practice how to be Giraffe-like—to speak their truth in honest, dignified words.

- Challenge kids to consider and discuss why using different response styles, like the Zookeeper, might be preferable for specific situations. For example, if the person who is bullying is normally friendly, perhaps responding with humor or changing the subject (characteristic of a Butterfly) would be the best option, whereas with a person who is persistently cruel, reaching out to an adult for help (a Wolf trait) would be more effective.
- Ask kids to develop their own two- to three-question Bully-Busting Quiz for you or for their peers. This exercise is very helpful in getting kids to think through realistic scenarios they encounter in their daily lives and to carefully consider the varied choices they can make in responding. Allow kids to walk you through each response option and lead a discussion about the likely outcomes and consequences of each choice.

KEY 2

Connect With People You Trust

ACTIVITY 6 Is It Tattling or Is It Telling?

In the first two Activities of their workbook, kids read about the 3 P's of bullying behavior and learned that young people who bully aim to make others feel **P**owerless. Then, in Activity 5, kids learned that one of the best ways to hold on to power is to connect with others—just as a Wolf relies on the strength of his pack.

For many young people, the fear of being called a "tattletale" for telling an adult about a bullying situation is a deal-breaker in and of itself. The young people I talk to repeatedly tell me that they'd rather let a bully get away with hurting them than risk making the bullying worse by telling an adult.

I know that their fears are grounded in experience. I always acknowledge for kids this very real dilemma. Yet I also help young people realize that creating this sense of fear and shame about talking to an adult is exactly how a bully robs kids of their **P**ower. No child should live in fear, and no adult should allow this intimidation and isolation to go on unchecked. Activities 6 and 7 are devoted to helping you—and the young people in your life—know the difference between being a tattletale and being someone who is courageous and powerful enough to reach out to adults and tell them when their help is needed.

WHAT KIDS LEARN

Confusion over the differences between tattling and telling is very common, but it can become dangerous when it leads to important information not being shared. Since parents, teachers, counselors, and other adults can help with a problem only if they know it exists, kids need to understand when to tell them.

In this lesson, kids learn 6 *Simple Rules* about the most important differences between tattling and telling. Young people are encouraged to post the *6 Simple Rules* on the refrigerator at home, in their binder at school, or anywhere they can access them easily for a quick reminder. The more familiar kids become with the *6 Rules*, the easier it will be for them to make the right decision when a bullying situation occurs.

Tattling or Telling?
6 SIMPLE RULES

IT'S TATTLING IF	IT'S TELLING IF
1. No one is hurt or injured.	**1.** Someone is hurt and needs help.
2. The person did it by accident and is sorry.	**2.** The person did it on **P**urpose to be mean.
3. This is the first time something like this has happened.	**3.** There is a **P**attern to what is going on. Nothing you have done has stopped it.
4. You have the power to solve this on your own.	**4.** You don't have the **P**ower to solve this without an adult's help.
5. Your goal is to get someone in trouble.	**5.** Your goal is to keep someone safe.
6. It's a "So what?" problem.	**6.** It's a "This matters!" problem.

USING THE *6 SIMPLE RULES*

Directions:

Read the following questions. Write down your answers in the space provided. Talk over your thoughts with an adult you can trust.

1. Now that you know the difference between tattling and telling:

   a. Tell about a time when you or someone you know TATTLED.

   _____

   _____

   b. Tell about a time when you or someone you know made the smart decision
      to TELL an adult about a bullying situation:

   _____

   _____

2. Read the 2 situations below. In the space provided, write down whether you
   think the situation is a "So What?" problem or a "This Matters!" problem.

(This *Companion Guide* provides the correct answer in the
space below. The *Activity Book* does not.)

Situation 1:

*Jonathan and Missy are chasing each other on the playground at
recess. Missy gets tired. She tells Jonathan she doesn't want to
play anymore. Jonathan still wants to play. He asks Missy, "What
are you, a sissy?" He gets all the boys to yell, "Missy is a sissy!*

Missy is a sissy!" Missy gets so mad that she starts chasing Jonathan. When she catches him, she punches him in the stomach. She says, "Would a sissy hit like that?" Jonathan's holds his stomach and whispers, "I can't breathe!"

This is a **THIS MATTERS!** problem that needs an adult's help.

Situation 2:

Jonathan and Missy are chasing each other on the playground at recess. Missy gets tired. She tells Jonathan she doesn't want to play anymore. Jonathan still wants to play. He asks Missy, "What are you, a sissy?" Missy looks Jonathan in the eye. She says, "I'm not a sissy, but I do need to catch my breath for a minute. I'll tell you when I'm ready to play again."

This is a **SO WHAT?** problem that the kids have worked out on their own.

WHAT ADULTS NEED TO KNOW

One of the most insidious aspects of bullying is how it makes young people feel isolated and alone (Whitson, 2014). Kids who are bullied are often hesitant to talk about their experiences because of the fear of being called a "tattletale" or "narc" and because of their own self-doubt; many kids worry that to tell an adult about their victimization experiences would be to openly expose a part of themselves that feels inadequate.

These worries can make confiding in an adult about bullying quite scary. It is our responsibility to make it feel safe. Key 2 of the *8 Keys to End Bullying* book explores ways in which adults can make it easier for kids to talk about bullying. A brief summary of effective strategies is provided here:

HOW TO RESPOND TO A CHILD WHO TALKS ABOUT BULLYING

1. Listen well. Make it a habit to show calm as you let the child tell his story.
2. Give kids your complete attention and focus when they are talking to you about bullying.
3. Keep an open mind and rid yourself of any already-drawn conclusions about the situation.
4. Use open-ended questions, as needed, to prompt a child to tell his or her story.
5. Show support, empathy, and compassion for a young person's feelings and experiences.
6. Help establish safe reporting methods so that kids can talk to adults without fear of retaliation and life getting worse.

TIPS TO HELP KIDS UNDERSTAND THE ACTIVITY

- Talk to kids about the differences between tattling and telling using the terms and *6 Simple Rules* provided in the Activity. Check to make sure the young person genuinely understands why it's vital that young people reach out to adults for support in handling bullying.
- Challenge kids to think about a time when they tattled on someone else:
  ◊ What did they tattle about?
  ◊ To whom did they tattle?
  ◊ What did they hope to have happen after they tattled?

◊ Now that they know the *6 Rules*, what could they have done instead of tattling?

- Encourage discussion about a time when a child told an adult about a bullying situation:
  ◊ What happened?
  ◊ Whom did they tell?
  ◊ Was the adult willing/able to help them handle the bullying?
  ◊ If so, what did the adult do?
  ◊ Did the bullying stop? Why or why not?
- Highlight Rule 6 for kids. Challenge them to explain in their own words the difference between a "So What?" issue and a "This Matters!" issue.
- If you are working with kids in a school or community setting, assign each young person to write down two scenarios—one that represents tattling and one that represents telling.
  ◊ Collect all the scenarios and then redistribute them so that each child has a written scenario to read.
  ◊ Have the children take turns reading their scenario aloud, then ask for volunteers to try to identify whether the scenario represents tattling or telling.
  ◊ Encourage group discussion about each scenario.

ACTIVITY 7 Tattling or Telling? 6 Simple Rules

In this activity, young people are challenged to apply the 6 *Simple Rules* about tattling vs. telling to everyday life. Below, you will find the 16 scenarios that kids read in their *Activity Book* accompanied by their correct classification. On the following page, you are provided with a rationale for each response that can guide you in engaging kids about the key differences between tattling and telling. This *Companion Guide* also includes four brand-new scenarios—not provided in the *Activity Book for Kids & Tweens*—for additional discussion.

WHAT KIDS LEARN

In the activity on pages 42–43, you'll use the *6 Simple Rules* to tell the difference between TATTLING and TELLING situations.

Materials Needed:

- 1 red crayon or pencil

- 1 green crayon or pencil

- A copy of **Tattling or Telling? 6 Simple Rules**

Tattling or Telling?

Directions:

Read each statement below. Each is something that a young person might say to an adult. If you think the situation is an example of tattling, color it **red**. If you think it is an example of telling, color it **green**.

Jessica just picked her nose. **TATTLING**

Olivia won't share the jump rope with me. **TATTLING**

Ella keeps locking Jennie in the bathroom. **TELLING**

Those three 5th-grade girls keep calling Carlos a baby when he walks by. **TELLING**

Ainsleigh grabbed Ava's test paper. She held it up so everyone could see Ava got 10 questions wrong. **TELLING**

Nicole started a text rumor that Katrina and Ethan kissed. She sent it to the whole class! **TELLING**

Sasha butted in front of me in line. **TATTLING**

Lily copied Brady's homework. **TATTLING**

Connor is throwing rocks at the girls on the swings. **TELLING**

Elijah trips Ariana every day when she's trying to get off the bus. **TELLING**

Kevin said I was the slowest runner in the whole 4th grade. **TATTLING**

Dylan is bragging that he's the best reader in the whole class. **TATTLING**

Sophie told all the girls not to play with Caitlyn at recess. **TELLING**

Colin deleted the characters on my video game by accident. **TATTLING**

Fiona promised she would play with me at recess, but now she's playing with other people. **TATTLING**

Kelly got hit in the head with a dodgeball. Now she says she feels dizzy. **TELLING**

Following the activity, kids are provided with the Answer Key for the *Tattling or Telling? 6 Simple Rules* activity. They are invited to compare their answers with the ones provided below.

Tattling or Telling?
6 Simple Rules Answer Key

TATTLING BEHAVIORS (These behaviors should be shaded red on page 42–43 of your book.)	TELLING BEHAVIORS (These behaviors should be shaded green on page 42–43 of your book.)
Jessica just picked her nose.	Ella keeps locking Jennie in the bathroom.
Olivia won't share the jump rope with me.	Sophie told all the girls not to play with Caitlyn at recess.
Kevin said I was the slowest runner in the whole 4th grade.	Elijah trips Ariana every day when she's trying to get off the bus.
Sasha butted in front of me in line.	Connor is throwing rocks at the girls on the swings.
Lily copied Brady's homework.	Those three 5th-grade girls keep calling Carlos a baby when he walks by.
Dylan is bragging that he's the best reader in the whole class.	Nicole started a text rumor that Katrina and Ethan kissed. She sent it to the whole class!
Fiona promised she would play with me at recess, but now she's playing with other people.	Kelly got hit in the head with a dodgeball. Now she says she feels dizzy.
Colin deleted the characters on my video game by accident.	Ainsleigh grabbed Ava's test paper. She held it up so everyone could see Ava got 10 questions wrong.

Some of your responses may not match the ones in the Answer Key. Don't mark them wrong! Instead, talk with a helpful adult about the *6 Simple Rules*. Explain why you chose red or green for each one. Talking about the *6 Simple Rules* with others is one of the best ways to learn and understand them.

 IN THE SPACE BELOW, write 1 example of tattling and 1 example of telling. Challenge a brother, sister, friend, parent, teacher, or other adult to identify your examples. Have them use the *6 Simple Rules* as a guide!

TIPS TO HELP KIDS UNDERSTAND THE ACTIVITY

- Keep in mind that the answers listed in the Answer Key on page 46 are not exhaustive. In many of the scenarios, for example, we don't have enough information to truly know whether or not there is a purpose or pattern to the behavior. Speculation about these matters, however, is valuable and productive fodder for conversation with young people.

- A priority of the activity is to help young people gain insights into when they are unnecessarily tattling on a sibling or peer versus when they are telling an adult important information that he needs in order to improve the situation. Most important, the goal is to empower kids to reach out to trustworthy adults without embarrassment, fear, or shame.

- Encourage kids to talk about past problem situations in their life in which they were unsure about whether or not to talk to an adult. Use the *6 Simple Rules* as a guide to help kids determine if reaching out in each situation would have been helpful or not.

- *Companion Guide* readers are provided with ADDITIONAL SCENARIOS (below) to challenge kids to think even more about key differences between tattling and telling:

◊ Jeff turned off the power on the classroom computer instead of logging off. (Tattling. Rules 1 & 5 apply.)

◊ Lucy handed out birthday party invitations to every girl in class except Marcie. (Telling. Rules 2, 3, & 4 apply.)

◊ Payton told me that if I try out for the field hockey team, she'll text everyone that I was cut from the soccer team. (Telling. Rules 2 & 4 apply.)

◊ Damon told Madeline that he didn't want to sit with her on the bus because he was saving a seat for his little sister. (Tattling. Rules 1, 5, & 6 apply.)

ACTIVITY 8 Who Can You Talk to About Bullying?

In this Activity, readers learn about and draft their very own Safety Plan that identifies *who* to talk to and *what* facts to provide about an incident of bullying. Kids also learn *why* the timing of their report is important and *how* they can remain anonymous when reporting bullying.

WHAT KIDS LEARN

By now, you know that asking for help when you see bullying is never a sign of weakness. Connecting with others is one of the most **p**owerful and brave things you can do. This next activity gives you the chance to make a **Safety Plan**. This plan will help you be prepared if you are involved in or find out about bullying.

KEY POINT

Some kids think that grown-ups won't do anything to stop bullying. Why should they even tell them about it? The truth, though, is that adults can't do anything if they don't know there is a problem. So make it your job to let them know!

INSTRUCTIONS FOR COMPLETING THE **SAFETY PLAN**:

QUESTION 1 asks you to list 3 adults that would help you handle a bullying situation. For this part of your Safety Plan, be sure to choose grown-ups who:

✓ Are good listeners. They take their time to really hear you when you ask them for help.

✓ You trust. Avoid an adult that would tell others that you are their source of information.

✓ Will take you seriously. Look for someone who understands that bullying is way more than just "kids being kids."

✓ Are able to stop the bullying. Your favorite aunt who lives 1,000 miles away may be a great listener. She may be trustworthy and take you seriously. But if she doesn't live close enough to actually help stop the bullying, be sure to add other adults to your list.

QUESTION 2 asks you what you'll do if these adults do not end up giving you the help you need:

✓ Don't give up! Yes, there are adults who don't pay attention to reports of bullying. Sadly, some adults get so busy with other things that they forget all about your report. But there are even more adults who care about you and want to keep you safe. *Keep talking until you find your champion who will help you!*

✓ Talk to your parents. Consider all your teachers, including teachers for Art, Music, Gym, and Music. Go to your School Counselor. Go to the principal. Go to your bus driver. Go to a coach or a youth group leader outside of school. Keep at it until you find someone who will believe you and truly help.

QUESTION 3 asks you to focus on the most important details of the bullying.

✓ Keep in mind that bullying will bring up lots of strong *feelings* in you. To really help change a situation, an adult will need to know the *facts* of what is going on. Try to keep your feelings under control.

✓ In the "What happened?" section, try to list the events in the order they happened. Include as much detail as possible.

✓ Even if you, or someone you know, chose a not-so-good response to bullying, be honest in telling an adult the full story so that they can help you.

QUESTION 4 asks you to record the date(s) and time(s) of the bullying.

✓ A common mistake kids make when dealing with bullying is to ignore it and hope it will go away. Remember: Bullying is a **P**attern of behavior that does not stop by itself. In fact, it usually just gets worse and worse over time! That's why it's important to connect with an adult before someone is badly hurt.

QUESTION 5 asks you to think about how you might make an *anonymous* report about bullying.

✓ Always remember that going to an adult in school or telling your parents about bullying is a sign of strength. You are not a tattletale. You are not a crybaby. *You are smart and brave.*

✓ Some schools have anonymous reporting forms on their website. Find out if your school has this.

✓ Other schools have phone numbers kids can use to make anonymous calls or texts about bullying.

✓ Does your school have an "Information" box where kids can leave anonymous notes about bullying?

✓ Keep in mind that you can tell an adult about bullying and ask them not to use your name. When a trustworthy adult does not tell others your name, this is called a *confidential* report.

✓ Keep in mind that you can tell an adult about bullying and ask them not to use your name. When a trustworthy adult does not tell others your name, this is called a *confidential* report.

Information Box

_____'s   Safety Plan

1. List 3 adults who would help you handle a bullying situation.

   _____

   _____

   _____

2. Who else will you talk to if these adults do not take your report of bullying seriously or do not try to help you?

   _____

   _____

   _____

3. Before telling an adult about bullying, focus on the most important details, as best as you can remember them. Write down:
   Who was involved in the situation? _____
   Where did the bullying take place? _____
   What happened?

   _____

   _____

   _____

4. When did the bullying happen?
   Date (s): _____
   Time (s): _____
   Has this ever happened before? If so, when? _____

5. You can choose to tell an adult in person about the bullying, or you may include the information from Questions 3 and 4 in an anonymous or confidential report. How will you report the bullying?
   ☐ Tell an adult in person
   ☐ Use my school's anonymous website form
   ☐ Use my school's confidential phone number or text system
   ☐ Use my school's anonymous information box
   ☐ Other: _____

WHAT ADULTS NEED TO KNOW

Once we have prepared young people for *when* to reach out to adults and *how* to safely report bullying, the next challenge is one that lands squarely in our laps. As adults, we need to know *how to respond well* to young people so that they know that the risk they took in reaching out to us was worthwhile.

Knowing what to say and do can be a challenge, however. It's not uncommon for parents, family members, teachers, and even counselors to be at a loss for words when kids tell us about troubling dynamics or incidents of cruelty. In Key 2 of the *8 Keys to End Bullying* book, five steps for responding well to a child's report of bullying are explained. These steps are summarized below for your reference:

1. Maintain calm. Communicate to kids that their problem is manageable.
2. Express sympathy for what the child has been going through.
3. Thank the child for having the courage to reach out to you for help.
4. Encourage the child to problem-solve the best way(s) to handle the bullying.
5. Follow up with the child on a regular basis to ensure that the situation is improving.

TIPS TO HELP KIDS UNDERSTAND THE ACTIVITY

- Encourage kids to share their written Safety Plan with you. Talk about each element, including:
  - ◊ Why each of the adults they identified in Questions 1 and 2 is considered trustworthy and what they anticipate each adult may be able to do to help.
    - If you are not identified as one of the trustworthy adults in a child's Safety Plan, do not allow yourself to be offended or put off. Kids

choose specific adults for particular reasons, and it's important that we honor their ideas.

- If you would like to be added to the list, tell the child and request that she add your name. This can be a great opportunity to communicate to a young person that you have their back and will support her if she ever needs you.
- If you recognize a name on the list that you consider an untrustworthy adult, resist the urge to say so. Putting down one of the child's choices may only alienate the child or cause unnecessary doubt. As long as there are multiple adults listed, the child should be in good shape.

◊ Why writing down facts is an important strategy for ensuring that details are remembered fully and reported accurately.

◊ Why it's so important for kids to take action to stop bullying when the problem is still manageable rather than waiting until a problem is out of control or someone is hurt.

◊ Options for anonymous and confidential reporting.

- Be sure that kids understand the difference between an anonymous report and a confidential one. Definitions for each term are provided in the Activity itself as well as in the Glossary of the *Activity Book.*
- Help kids identify the best reporting method for their situation.

- Talk about a real-life or realistic bullying situation with a child. Challenge the child to write out a safety plan for the situation. Discuss the plan and its likely outcomes with him.

- Offer to make photocopies of the Safety Plan for the child so that a draft can be used as part of your discussions and extra copies remain for real-life situations that occur.

ACTIVITY 9 Finding Fun Friendships

Have you ever heard the expression, "Cast a wide net?" When kids put effort into getting to know all kinds of different peers from all sorts of different places, they give themselves lots of options for making friends with similar interests and hobbies. One of the best things you can do to protect a young person you care about from the loneliness and isolation caused by bullying is to give him opportunities to connect with loyal, fun, true friendships in a range of settings.

WHAT KIDS LEARN

Anaya is the tallest kid in the 5th grade. Every day, she gets made fun of for her long, skinny legs and huge feet. In her neighborhood, on the other hand, she is known for being a star swimmer and great teammate. Every kid from her youth group wants her to try out for basketball. Her best friend from her old neighborhood texts with her every day after school.

Maybe you know someone like Anaya. Maybe you understand just how Anaya feels because you have had a tough time making friends at school. The truth is that bullying usually has very little to do with the person being bullied and everything to do with certain people in certain groups.

The good news is that by "casting a wide net" and finding fun friendships beyond just your class in school, you can light up the dark spaces left by not-so-nice kids elsewhere. The next Activity is designed to get you thinking about your likes, strengths, hobbies, talents, and skills so that you can connect with kids who help you feel great.

30 QUESTIONS FOR KIDS

Directions:

Use these questions (and your answers to them!) to think about the types of groups you'd like to join. Exploring activities and interests that help you feel good about yourself is a key to finding fun friendships.

1. The nicest thing anyone has ever said to me is:
    _____

2. When I grow up, I want to be a:
    _____

3. I like to collect:
    _____

4. My top 3 favorite movies are:
    _____

5. My lucky number is:
    _____

6. Something I've always wanted to learn to do is:
    _____

7. 4 words I use to describe myself are:
    _____

8. An ideal friend is someone who:
    _____

9. The best app I've ever used is:
    _____

10. The hardest thing I've ever had to do is:
    _____

11. My favorite sport to play is:

_____

12. My favorite sport to watch is:

_____

13. If I could travel in time, I would visit:

_____

14. When I have free time, I love to:

_____

15. If I was president for a month, I would:

_____

16. The thing I am best at is:

_____

17. My favorite ice cream flavor is:

_____

18. The coolest place I have ever been is:

_____

19. If I could pick any superpower, I'd pick:

_____

20. Someday, I want to invent:

_____

21. If I were in a band, I would play:

_____

22. When I am feeling sad, what helps me start to feel better is:

_____

23. If I had 10 million dollars, I would:

_____

24. My favorite song is:

_____

25. I do / do not (*circle one*) like having pets because:

_____

26. I make other people laugh when I:

_____

27. One thing that makes me really proud of myself is:

_____

28. A positive change I made about myself was:

_____

29. The thing that scares me the most is:

_____

30. The best thing about being me is:

_____

KEY POINT

Did you notice that none of the questions on the list are about race, politics, religion, or the amount of money your family has? That's because these things are not important when it comes to making friends. *Never let the differences between you and someone else keep you from becoming friends.* Remember that it's easy to become friends with people who live very differently when you have the same interests, hobbies, or skills.

- Use the **30 Questions for Kids** with a friend.
  - Ask your friend each question, then compare your answers.
  - This is a fun way to get to know someone. Share laughs as you talk about your answers!
- Consider using the **30 Questions** with a whole group of kids.
  - Try to guess who wrote which answer.
  - You'll learn new things about people you thought you knew well. Besides, it's a lot of fun trying to figure out who said what!

WHAT ADULTS NEED TO KNOW

For some young people, establishing peer connections comes as naturally as breathing; for others, the process is confusing and confounding. Providing young people with multiple opportunities to engage with and connect to peers who share their interests, hobbies, strengths, and even quirks is a critically important way to reduce a child's social isolation. When young people know that there are adults and kids whom they can reach out to and who accept them for who they are, they become less vulnerable to the loneliness and sense of powerlessness brought on by bullying.

This activity is a self-awareness tool, designed to help young people focus on their likes, strengths, interests, and aspirations. By discovering these qualities through a fun, engaging Q&A activity, kids gain insight into extracurricular activities to explore and peers with whom they could connect.

TIPS TO HELP KIDS UNDERSTAND THE ACTIVITY

- Encourage kids to use the *30 Questions* with a friend.
  - ◊ Kids can each write down their responses, then compare them.
  - ◊ Alternatively, they can take turns asking each other the questions.
  - ◊ Either way, this is a fun, nonthreatening way for young people to get to know each other and to laugh together as responses are shared.
- Consider using the *30 Questions* with a group of kids. After each child records her responses, challenge group member to guess who wrote which answer.
  - ◊ Young people will learn new things about peers they thought they knew well and have fun trying to figure out who said what.
  - ◊ Add or edit questions from the list based on your particular group's age, interests, needs, etc.
- An important issue for consideration is also the questions that are *not* on the list. Initiate a conversation with kids about the following:
  - ◊ Did you notice that none of the questions on the list have anything to do with race, ethnicity, politics, religion, or the amount of money your family has?
  - ◊ Emphasize that these qualities and beliefs are not important in determining the quality of the friendships kids can make.
  - ◊ Prompt young people: *Never let your differences from someone else be a barrier to becoming friends.*
  - ◊ Encourage kids to always remember that it's easy to become friends with people who live with very different circumstances when interests and hobbies are shared.
- Engage young people in reflecting on the following questions about positive friendships:
  - ◊ What are the qualities you look for in a friend?
  - ◊ When meeting a group of kids for the first time, what draws you toward trying to make friends with someone?

◊ Do you tend to seek out kids who have similar interests to you, or are you more likely to be drawn to kids you consider popular?

◊ What is the difference between being *popular* and being *well-liked*? Which is more important to you? Why?

◊ Explain how the process of making a friend works for you and whether or not you think your way of making friends is working out well.

◊ If not, what could you do differently when making friends?

Stop Bullying Whenever You See It

ACTIVITY 10 Words Matter

Words matter. In this activity, young people learn that the words they use have a major effect on how other people feel. Kids learn important differences between "cotton" words that build strong friendships and "sandpaper" words that wear away at relationships.

Whenever possible, *Companion Guide* readers are asked to support kids in this Activity by providing actual samples of cotton and sandpaper for young people to touch and to compare. The long-term learning in this activity is greatly enhanced by this hands-on component. Touching the cotton and sandpaper provides a sensory experience for kids, which makes it an especially memorable lesson for learning standards of kindness at home, at school, and in their community.

WHAT KIDS LEARN

First, kids learn that the old "sticks and stones" rhyme really doesn't hold water. Anyone who has ever been called a cruel name or been yelled at by a friend knows that words really can—and often do—cause quite a bit of emotional pain! To really get a *feel* for this concept, kids are prompted to try this sensory experiment:

EXPERIMENT

Step 1: Take the cotton ball in your hand. Move it between your fingers. Notice how it feels on your skin.

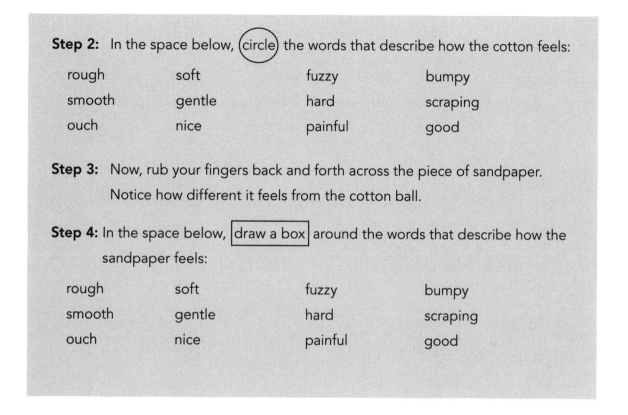

Step 2: In the space below, (circle) the words that describe how the cotton feels:

rough	soft	fuzzy	bumpy
smooth	gentle	hard	scraping
ouch	nice	painful	good

Step 3: Now, rub your fingers back and forth across the piece of sandpaper. Notice how different it feels from the cotton ball.

Step 4: In the space below, draw a box around the words that describe how the sandpaper feels:

rough	soft	fuzzy	bumpy
smooth	gentle	hard	scraping
ouch	nice	painful	good

Kids learn that words can be a lot like cotton and sandpaper. Some words make kids feel warm and fuzzy like cotton, while other words are rough like sandpaper and can hurt kids' feelings. "Cotton words" are further defined as compliments, good manners, or giving encouragement to others, while "sandpaper words" are described as terms used to insult, mock, threaten, tease, or tattle on others. Kids are then challenged to list real-life examples of cotton and sandpaper words and to describe how they feel when these types of words are spoken.

In the next activity, provided below, kids practice choosing between cotton and sandpaper words.

Cotton & Sandpaper

Directions:

Read each statement below. Circle "Cotton" if the statement represents warm, kind words. Circle "Sandpaper" if the statement is an example of rough or bullying language.

1.	Please stop calling me names.	Cotton	Sandpaper
2.	You're calling me names! You're mean.	Cotton	Sandpaper
3.	I'm sorry I bumped into you. It was an accident.	Cotton	Sandpaper
4.	It's so embarrassing when you tell people my secrets. Will you please keep them to yourself?	Cotton	Sandpaper
5.	If you don't stop, I'm going to take your Legos!	Cotton	Sandpaper
6.	You butted in line. I'm telling on you!	Cotton	Sandpaper
7.	I asked you to stop touching me, but you're not listening. If you do it again, I am going to ask the teacher for help.	Cotton	Sandpaper
8.	Can I please play with you guys?	Cotton	Sandpaper
9.	I can't see! Get out of my way!	Cotton	Sandpaper
10.	Can you please sit down so I can see?	Cotton	Sandpaper
11.	Please stop laughing at me.	Cotton	Sandpaper
12.	I'm not your friend anymore!	Cotton	Sandpaper
13.	You can't play with us!	Cotton	Sandpaper
14.	You cheated! I hate you.	Cotton	Sandpaper
15.	Give me that back! It's mine!	Cotton	Sandpaper

Do you know the difference between cotton and sandpaper words? An Answer Key is provided at the end of this Activity for you to check your responses.

WHAT ADULTS NEED TO KNOW

It's common in elementary and middle schools for kids to become known for specific talents, abilities, and personality traits. Some kids are known for being great artists or star athletes. Others are recognized for playing an instrument, shining on stage, or getting straight A's.

As a parent, teacher, counselor, or other caring adult, you play an important role in encouraging kids to make it their goal to *be known for being kind* in addition to the recognition they get for artistic, academic, or athletic endeavors.

Choosing cotton words and avoiding sandpaper words is a great way for young people to gain skills for forming positive friendships. Likewise, for kids who often seem drawn to negative peers or who get involved in relationships with manipulative peers, the ability to readily recognize "sandpaper" words when a peer is using them can signal to the child that the particular friendship is not a healthy one for them to pursue.

TIPS TO HELP KIDS UNDERSTAND THE ACTIVITY

- Discuss the title of this activity with your young person. Challenge him or her to explain in their own words why "words matter" so much when it comes to communicating and connecting with peers.
- In addition to providing actual samples of cotton and sandpaper for young people to touch and to compare, help youngsters brainstorm examples of "cotton" words that are used to make others feel good as well as "sandpaper" words that put others down.
- If you are teaching this lesson to a school or community group, consider

providing a cotton ball for each child to take home as a tangible reminder to use kind words as often as possible.

- Review the *Cotton & Sandpaper* worksheet with kids. Encourage discussion about why each response was selected. If any of the child's answers do not correspond with those provided in the Answer Key (below), do not consider it wrong necessarily, but rather engage the child in a conversation about how the words can be used to either help or hurt someone.

- In Activity 12, kids will learn how their tone of voice can either support or change the meaning of the words they use. You can use the phrases in the *Cotton & Sandpaper* worksheet to pre-teach the importance of tone of voice, as follows:

  ◊ Read the first statement, "Please stop calling me names," aloud in a polite, calm tone to confirm that these are typically "cotton" words.

  ◊ Reread the same statement, but this time, read it (or yell it) in a loud, gruff, angry voice.

  ◊ Talk to kids about how altering your tone of voice can change the whole meaning of a phrase—and turn a cotton phrase into a sandpaper one.

  ◊ Encourage kids to take the lead on doing this for several additional statements from the worksheet. Explain that tone of voice will be reviewed in more depth in Activity 12.

This Activity has been adapted for use in this workbook from "Cotton vs. sandpaper words," https://theschoolcounselorkind.wordpress.com/2013/12/26/cotton-vs-sandpaper-words/. Used by permission of the author.

Cotton and Sandpaper Words

A N S W E R   K E Y

1. Please stop calling me names.   (Cotton)   Sandpaper

2. You're calling me names! You're mean.   Cotton   (Sandpaper)

3. I'm sorry I bumped into you. It was an accident.   (Cotton)   Sandpaper

4. It's so embarrassing when you tell people my secrets.   (Cotton)   Sandpaper
   Will you please keep them to yourself?

5. If you don't stop, I'm going to take your Legos!   Cotton   (Sandpaper)

6. You butted in line. I'm telling on you!   Cotton   (Sandpaper)

7. I asked you to stop touching me, but you're not listening.   (Cotton)   Sandpaper
   If you do it again, I am going to ask the teacher for help.

8. Can I please play with you guys?   (Cotton)   Sandpaper

9. I can't see! Get out of my way!   Cotton   (Sandpaper)

10. Can you please sit down so I can see?   (Cotton)   Sandpaper

11. Please stop laughing at me.   (Cotton)   Sandpaper

12. I'm not your friend anymore!   Cotton   (Sandpaper)

13. You can't play with us!   Cotton   (Sandpaper)

14. You cheated! I hate you.   Cotton   (Sandpaper)

15. Give me that back! It's mine!   Cotton   (Sandpaper)

ACTIVITY 11 QUIZ TIME: What's My Reply?

In Activity 10, kids learned that *words matter* when it comes to connecting with others and forming good friendships. In this activity, young people will learn about the style of words that is most effective for replying to bullying.

WHAT KIDS LEARN

When it comes to getting dressed each day, we all have our own style. Some kids like to wear sporty clothing, while others prefer to dress up. For many, accessories rule; cool hats, glittery headbands, funny T-shirts, and interesting shoes are a must.

The truth is, a young person's style isn't limited to the clothing that he or she wears. Kids also express personal style each and every day by the way they respond to others. When it comes to handling a bullying situation, a young person's "Reply Style" goes a long way in determining how quickly the bullying ends—or how long it continues.

In Activity 11, reprinted below for your reference, kids are challenged to read each real-life situation and select the reply they think would be best for stopping bullying behavior. At the end of the quiz, information is provided about effective styles for stopping bullying.

What's My Reply?

1. You are working on a computer at school when a classmate comes over and says, "It's my turn!" He puts his hand on the back of your chair and starts to slide it out from the desk. You can no longer reach the keyboard. You:

   A. Shove him away and shout, "If you touch my chair again, I'll hit you!"
   B. Get up right away and give him the computer, even though you're not done with your work.
   C. Look him in the eye and say, "Please don't push my chair. You can have the computer as soon as I save my work."

2. On the bus home from school, a kid throws your book bag out of the back seat, saying that it's reserved for "5th-graders only." You tell her:

   A. "The 5th-graders are the biggest losers in the whole school!"
   B. "Okay, sorry."
   C. "I didn't know this seat was reserved. Next time, please tell me instead of throwing my stuff."

3. Kayla used to be your best friend. Lately, though, she's been hanging around with Abby. She barely talks to you anymore. This morning, she is extra nice to you and then says, "Can I copy your math homework? I forgot to do it last night!" You reply:

   A. "Yeah, right. Now you want to be my friend again? Go ask Abby, since you like her so much more than you like me!"

B. "Sure, Kayla."

C. "I would, but I don't want to get in trouble. I can explain it to you if you need help."

4. Out of the blue, Jonah texts you this message: "No one likes you. Why do you even come to school? You should just be homeschooled!" You:

A. Text a note to everyone in your class that says, "Jonah is the biggest loser in school. He'll never have a girlfriend because he is so ugly."

B. Start to cry, then delete the message before your mom or dad see it.

C. Take a screen shot of the text and show it to your teacher at school. Then block Jonah from texting you anymore.

5. You and Nolan are playing video games at your house after school. Nolan gets upset because you win 3 games in a row. He throws down his controller and says, "It's not fair! You're cheating!" You reply:

A. "Don't be such a whiny baby, Nolan. I can't help it if you stink at video games."

B. "It's my fault, Nolan. I shouldn't have played so hard. We can say that you won that round."

C. "I can tell you're not having fun anymore. Let's play something else. Just be careful of my controller—I don't want you to break my things."

What's My Reply? Quiz Choices:

Look back on the answers you chose for each of the 5 situations above:

In each of the situations, the "A" response shows MEAN behavior.
Just like the Tiger responses from Activity 5, *Mean* responses may be a natural instinct, but they are also a sure way to make a conflict worse. Plus, have you ever noticed that adults usually notice the person who reacted with Mean behavior before they realize that someone else started it? Be smart in your replies to others. Never confuse feeling better for a moment with solving a problem once and for all!

In each of the situations, the "B" response shows MEEK behavior.
"Meek" rhymes with "weak." Sadly, people who use Meek words—such as saying sorry when it isn't their fault or letting others hurt them—are thought of as weak by kids who bully. This weakness gives bullies a green light to keep hurting their victims over and over again.

Some people choose Meek replies because they are trying to be nice. Others choose Meekness because they want to avoid a fight. While these are both good goals, remember that *being known for being kind* is not the same as allowing other people to hurt you. Standing up for yourself with the "Mean-It" behaviors described next is always the best way to stop bullying.

In each of the situations, the "C" response shows MEAN-IT behavior.
Mean-It replies let the other person know that you mean what you say and say what you mean. You speak in a way that is honest but still polite and kind. You do not hurt others with your Mean-It voice, and you do not allow them to continue to hurt you.

You can show someone that you really *Mean It* when you:

- Look the person straight in the eye
- Speak in a strong, even voice
- Use clear words to tell the person what you do or do not want to have happen.

KEY POINT

Remember: Kids who bully are not looking for a fair fight! Their goal is to have **P**ower over someone else. They are looking for kids who either overreact with *Mean* behavior or underreact with *Meekness*. **When you show that you Mean It, you pick the perfect reply for stopping bullying before it can ever really get started.**

WRITE ABOUT IT

In the space below, write your own What's My Reply? quiz question.

- First, describe a situation from your real life where someone used bullying behavior.
- Then, write down 3 choices—one *Mean*, one *Meek*, and one *Mean-It*—for how a person could reply.
- Challenge a family member or friend to take your quiz.
- Talk to them about their Reply Style. If they chose a *Mean* or *Meek* answer, help them think about how they could make a better choice to bring an end to the bullying.

QUIZ QUESTION:

_____

_____

_____

_____

REPLY CHOICES:

a. _____

b. _____

c. _____

WHAT ADULTS NEED TO KNOW

Throughout Key 3 of the _8 Keys to End Bullying_ book, adults learn strategies for effective intervention whenever they see or become aware that bullying has occurred. In addition to learning about anti-bullying legislation and guidelines for creating positive school cultures, readers learn specific skills for using assertive communication and "brief messages" to stop bullying. Activities 10 through 13 in the _Activity Book for Kids & Tweens_ are likewise designed to teach young people a set of skills for responding assertively in bullying situations.

Rather than using terms like _aggressive, passive,_ and _assertive_—terms that often turn kids off—the phrases _Mean, Meek,_ and _Mean-It_ are introduced in the "What's My Reply" quiz. These three terms will be used in the book from this point forward. Depending on your child's age, vocabulary, and tolerance for psychological terms, you may choose either set of terms to use when speaking with kids about reply styles.

As you use this *Companion Guide* to help young people develop skills for stopping bullying, consider your own reply style. As a role model for young people, how can you demonstrate *Mean-It* words on a regular basis?

TIPS TO HELP KIDS UNDERSTAND THE ACTIVITY

- Talk with kids about each style of communication. Encourage dialogue about which style they identified within the quiz and which style feels most natural to them.
  ◊ For kids who identify as having a *Mean* or *Meek* style when it comes to responding to bullying, help them think about how small changes in their replies can get them closer to a more effective *Mean-It* style.
- Ask specific questions to deepen their understanding of each reply style, such as:
  ◊ What are the advantages/disadvantages of each style?
  ◊ How could a Mean style make a bullying problem worse?
  ◊ How could a Meek style allow bullying to go on, unnoticed by adults?
  ◊ Why are Mean-It words the most successful in stopping bad situations from becoming worse?
- Have you ever used a *Mean* reply to bullying? If so, what happened?
- Have you ever used a *Meek* response? Describe the situation.
- How comfortable do you feel showing others that you *Mean It*? Is this direct style ever difficult for you?
- How would tone of voice affect a reply style?

◊ What happens when Mean words are spoken in a Meek voice?

◊ What would happen to a Mean-It message if it was spoken in a Mean or Meek voice?

- As an "extra" in this activity, kids are challenged to write their own "What's My Reply?" quiz question. Encourage kids to take on this challenge, then offer to take their quiz.

ACTIVITY 12 Mean, Meek, or Mean-It?

In the last activity, young people were introduced to the concepts of *Mean, Meek,* and *Mean-It* replies to bullying. Kids learned that people who use *Mean-It* words are usually the most successful in stopping bad situations from becoming worse. In this Activity, kids gain additional insights for understanding how tone of voice plays a key role in supporting reply styles and emphasizing (or undermining) words.

WHAT KIDS LEARN

Just as kids can lower their voices to a whisper in a library or raise their voices to cheer for a favorite team, this Activity helps them understand how they can control the tone of their voice to respond effectively to bullying. In the activity, summarized below, kids learn to use their voice as a tool for handling conflict and stopping bullying.

Kids are instructed to read each statement in the activity aloud three times. First, they are asked to use a *Mean* voice that expresses anger and aggression. Then, they are challenged to repeat the statement in a *Meek* voice that expresses fear, guilt, or sadness. Last, kids are directed to use a strong, confident *Mean-It* voice that expresses that they mean what they say and say what they mean.

To make this activity even more eye-opening, kids are challenged to try these extra steps:

- Use a tablet or smartphone to record yourself saying each statement aloud in the 3 different voices. Play back the recording to hear how each Reply Style sounds.
- Read the statements aloud to a parent, brother, sister, or trusted friend. Ask them to tell you how your tone of voice supports your words.

STATEMENTS

1. Please turn down the volume on the TV.

2. I didn't say you were upset.

3. Can you pass the pasta?

4. What did you say?

5. Excuse me.

6. Stop it.

7. What were you thinking when you did that?

8. I need your help.

9. I'd like you to stop saying that.

10. That's not funny.

MORE TO THINK ABOUT

> *(The correct answers are provided here for Companion Guide readers. Kids' Activity Book readers find the Answer Key at the end of the Activity.)*

1. How did the meaning of each statement change depending on the tone of voice you used? (Match the correct responses.)

A Mean voice made me seem: powerful and confident

A Meek voice made me seem: angry and unkind

A Mean-It voice made me seem: weak and scared

2. How do you think someone would respond to you if you said something in a *Mean* tone of voice? (Circle all that apply.)

(a.) The person might want to fight me.

b. The person might think I'm really nice.

(c.) The person might be scared and avoid me.

(d.) The person might tell a teacher on me.

3. How could using a *Meek* voice make a situation worse? (Circle all that apply.)

(a.) It could make the person think I am weak and easy to control.

(b.) It could make the person think I don't know how to stand up for myself.

c. It could make me look strong and respected.

d. It could make me look as if I am ready for a fight.

4. In your own words, explain why a *Mean-It* voice is best for stopping bullying.

There are many possible correct responses. If you wrote something like the sentences below, you are on the right track!

A Mean-It voice shows that you mean what you say and say what you mean. You do not hurt other people and do not allow them to hurt you.

- -

Companion Guide readers are encouraged to ask kids about their responses to each of the questions. There are no "right" or "wrong" answers necessarily; kids should feel free to explore the concepts based on personal experience. Helping adults can guide kids to consider new perspectives and points of view as needed.

WHAT ADULTS NEED TO KNOW

Too often, kids are taught *not* to speak up about their needs. Young girls, in particular, too often learn that in certain social settings, they should apologize for stating their opinions. Adults play a critical role in helping kids learn that it is OK for young people to mean what they say without hesitation or apology and that learning to do so confidently can help them become less vulnerable to bullying.

Companion Guide readers are truly the perfect audience to listen to kids repeat the statements from Activity 12 in their *Mean*, *Meek*, and *Mean-It* voices and to provide feedback on the way each voice is received.

TIPS TO HELP KIDS UNDERSTAND THE ACTIVITY

- Kids tend to thoroughly enjoy this activity, as it allows them the opportunity to use their voices in exaggerated, silly, and new ways while still learning valuable insights about the power of communication. Encourage kids to have fun with the activity, repeating each phrase multiple times and exploring how even small variations in tone can impact the meaning of a message.

- Challenge young people to generate original phrases and to read them in alternating *Mean*, *Meek*, and *Mean-It* Voices.
- Revisiting a theme from the previous Activity, ask kids to consider:
  - ◊ What happens when *Mean* words are spoken in a *Meek* voice?
  - ◊ In contrast, what happens when *Meek* words are spoken in a *Mean* voice?
  - ◊ If *Mean* words are spoken in a *Mean-It* voice, is the message still mean? Why or why not? Offer an original example.
  - ◊ What would happen to a *Mean-It* message if it was spoken in a *Mean* or *Meek* voice? Offer an original example.
- Provide access to a smartphone, tablet, or other digital recording device so that kids can record themselves saying each statement aloud in the three different voices. Watch the playback with kids and offer your own feedback on their voice, their body language, their words, and how all three come together to communicate one message.

ACTIVITY 13 What to Say in a Bullying Situation

Have you ever been in a situation where someone says or does something cruel to you and you freeze up? You want to say something clever to stand up for yourself or funny to break the tension, but instead, all you can come up with is a blank stare. Or maybe words do come to your mouth, but they end up being *Mean* or *Meek* responses that make your situation go from bad to worse. In this Activity, kids learn specific *Mean-It* phrases so that when an unexpected incident of drama or bullying occurs, they are prepared to respond well.

WHAT KIDS LEARN

In the *Activity Book*, kids learn that they always have *choices* when it comes to how to respond to conflict and bullying. The words young people use and the tone of voice they choose in responding to the cruelty of others plays an important role in determining how often (and how badly) they are bullied. Kids learn that having the ability to choose a helpful response means that they need never let a bully put them in a **P**owerless position. That's empowering!

In this Activity, kids learn another bit of wisdom: Kids who are good at acting as if a peer's hurtful comments or cruel behavior don't bother them are usually very successful at stopping bullying in its tracks (Laugeson, 2013). Using a scrambled word puzzle, readers learn 10 sample phrases that can be used to communicate to a would-be bully that his behavior is not cool.

An important reminder for readers in this Activity is that kids who bully feel **P**owerful when they get a big, emotional reaction from their targets (such as a *Mean* comeback or a *Meek* reply). When kids act like they couldn't care less about what a bully says, on the other hand, they effectively sap the bully's **P**ower and make it far less likely that he or she will target them again. In short, the phrases taught to kids in this Activity make bullying boring—which is a deal-breaker for power-seeking youth.

Mixed-Up Mean-It Comebacks

Directions:

Banish the "brain freeze" of being caught off guard by bullying! Never be at a loss for words again! Unscramble each of the phrases below to reveal a helpful comeback to bullying.

1. htW'as uory ontpi?   _____

2. oNt oolc.   _____

3. rateevhW   _____

4. h'Ttas os otn nynuf.   _____

5. fl oyu ays os.   _____

6. hTat dssnou ielk a mourr ot em.   _____

7. I eilk het ywa I ookl.   _____

8. yyAawn.   _____

9. kKcno ti fof.   _____

10. lelT em nweh ouy etg ot het nyufn tarp.   _____

An Answer Key is provided at the end of this Activity.

Now you know 10 new phrases for responding to bullying. Remember to say them in a *Mean-It* tone of voice. Look the person in the eye as you are speaking. These are simple but powerful actions. They tell others that you are strong. They let people knowing that continuing to taunt or bully you won't be any fun at all.

THE BEST COMEBACKS sound natural when you say them aloud. Are there any phrases from the Activity that do not seem like they would come out of your mouth? If so, that's okay! We all have our own way of speaking. If any of the phrases on the list sound strange to you, they won't sound real when you say them. In the space below, write down 3 to 4 original *Mean-It* comebacks that you will feel comfortable using in a bullying situation:

_____ _____

_____ _____

To get these comebacks to work even better, practice saying them in front of a mirror. Use a natural, *Mean-It* tone of voice. Better still, grab a brother. sister, friend, or parent. Practice saying these words out loud to them. Ask them what you could do to say them even better. Using the advice they give you will help you reply well in a real-life bullying situation.

WHAT ADULTS NEED TO KNOW

While it is a most effective approach for young people to act and respond as if they do not care about a bully's cruel words and deeds, the truth is that most kids feel the impact of bullying very deeply. Even if it is in a kid's best interests to put on a front of indifference in front of peers, it is critical that he have someone that he can be honest with about his real feelings about being bullied.

Be that person for a child.

Listen to his story, empathize with her feelings, believe what he is telling you, and help her whenever you can. Empower the young person with practical communication skills for coping with bullying, such as assertive (*Mean-It*) phrasing, supported by a strong (*Mean-It*) voice. Let each young person know that he is powerful beyond measure and can handle bullying by making good choices in his responses and courageous decisions to reach out to trustworthy adults.

TIPS TO HELP KIDS UNDERSTAND THE ACTIVITY

- Encourage discussion about why it might be that a child who bullies is looking for an emotional response from his target. Help kids to understand how a bully derives a sense of **P**ower from controlling someone else's reaction.
- Continue the conversation by challenging kids to consider why "making bullying boring" through controlled, nonemotional responses is so effective.
- In many ways, this is a lighthearted activity because of the scrambled words format. Yet the skills kids can gain from learning a handful of simple, easy-to-remember, unemotional, natural-sounding, assertive replies to bullying are invaluable. Encourage kids to share their thoughts on the 10 phrases used in the activity, as follows:

◊ Are there phrases on this list that you already typically use? If so, which ones?

◊ How do others respond when you use these phrases?

◊ Are there any phrases on the list that you can see yourself trying? Which ones?

◊ Are there any phrases that do not seem natural to you?

- Encourage kids to brainstorm three to four original *Mean-It* replies that they would feel comfortable using in a bullying situation.

- If you have your own suggestions for effective comebacks that *make bullying boring*, feel free to suggest them to kids. Ask for their feedback on the phrases you suggest.

- As a tie-in to Activity 12, provide access to a smartphone, tablet, or other digital recording device so that kids can record themselves saying each *Mean-It* statement aloud. Watch the playback with kids and offer your own feedback on their voice, their body language, their words, and how all three come together to communicate one assertive message.

Mixed-Up Mean-It Comebacks

A N S W E R   K E Y

1. What's your point?

2. Not cool.

3. Whatever.

4. That's so not funny.

5. If you say so.

6. That sounds like a rumor to me.

7. I like the way I look.

8. Anyway.

9. Knock it off.

10. Tell me when you get to the funny part.

Be Cyberbullying Free

ACTIVITY 14 What's Your Favorite App?

According to a study by the Pew Research Center, 92% of teens report going online every single day (Lenhart, 2015). More than half of the kids polled say they go online several times each day, and 24% admit to going online "almost constantly." Many young people head straight for popular social media sites and apps such as Instagram, Twitter, Snapchat, ASKfm, and Facebook, while texting with friends is a constant background activity. Talk about accomplished multitaskers!

Indeed, kids growing up in the early years of the 21st century are digital natives, and many times we, as the parents and professionals who care about them, feel like immigrants in our kids' native cyber-lands. Yet, throwing up our hands and surrendering to a young person's greater technological acumen is akin to letting a toddler go to the city playground all alone.

One of the most important things that adults can do for today's youth is maintain an informed awareness of digital culture and teach kids specific strategies and standards for safe, respectful online behavior. This *Companion Guide* empowers you to do just that as you follow along and follow up with kids on the interactive, insight-oriented, engaging exercises in their *Activity Book*.

Seven activities are offered to kids in this section of their workbook—more than in any other single section. This is a very intentional way of:

1. Acknowledging the huge impact that technology has on their lives
2. Celebrating all the fun ways that technology connects them with peers
3. Empowering kids to use smartphones, tablets, iPods, iPads, Apple watches, laptops, and other gadgets wisely.

In Activity 14, kids begin to thoughtfully consider their uses of technology by focusing on their favorite social media app, website, or video game and thinking through how technology impacts their friendships—for better and for worse.

WHAT KIDS LEARN

Do the adults in your life enjoy using technology as much as you do? Today, people of most ages own gadgets like smartphones, laptops, tablets, and gaming devices. Many of us use them several times each day—if not all day! And yet you may know adults who seem concerned about your use of gadgets. Why do you think the very adults who love their own technology get so concerned about your tech use?

The truth is, as handy and fun as technology is, it also creates real dangers for young people. Adults are right to have concerns, especially about safety, friendships, and bullying. There are ways you can assure adults that you are using your gadgets in safe, fun, respectful ways. One of the best ways is to show them that you understand their worries. Make it clear that you have thought through what is good and bad about your devices. The questions in this Activity are designed to help you do that.

GADGETS, GAMES, & **ME**

Directions:

Read each question below. Think carefully about your answer. In the space provided, write down your response.

Consider sharing your thoughts and ideas with a parent, relative, teacher, or other caring adult who can be there for you if you ever need help or advice.

1. What is your favorite app, website, or video game?

_____

_____

2. What do you like best about it?

_____

_____

3. About how often do you visit this app/site/game? (Circle the best answer.)

About once a month   About once a week   About once a day

A few times each month   A few times each week   A few times each day

4. Do you interact with your friends on this app/site/game? (Check one.)

☐ Yes, I like to play this game/app with others.

☐ No, this is an app/site/game I usually use alone.

5. Has using this app/site/game helped you become closer with certain friends?
Has it hurt any of your relationships? Explain.

_____

_____

6. How is this app/site/game used to cyberbully? (Check all that apply.)

☐ It isn't.

☐ People can post cruel comments.

☐ People can post embarrassing photos.

☐ People can post anonymously.

☐ People can forward messages or photos without the sender's permission.

☐ People can be kicked out of the chat/game on purpose.

☐ Other: _____

7. Have you ever seen people be cruel to each other on this app/site/game? What do you do if this happens?

_____

_____

8. Does this app/site/game ever add to your FOMO (fear of missing out?). If so, how? How do you handle it?

_____

_____

9. If you could create your own app, social media site, or video game, what would it be like? In the lined area below, give it a name. Describe it in your own words. Then, use the open space to sketch your creation's home screen.

NAME:

_____

DESCRIPTION:

_____

_____

_____

> NOTE TO COMPANION GUIDE READERS: In the *Activity Book*, young readers are also provided with the opportunity to design and sketch the home screen of the app, social media site, or game that they create. Please ask them about their sketch and encourage them to describe their creation to you.

WHAT ADULTS NEED TO KNOW

As parents and professionals, we are all too aware of the dangers posed by too much technology in the lives of our young people—from lack of physical exercise, underdeveloped social skills, and actual changes in brain development to distractions from academic work, vulnerability to online predators, sexual exploitation, and relentless cyberbullying (to name just a few.) Yet, we also know that if we approach kids with a soapbox-style lecture about all of these potential pitfalls, we will instantly seem out of touch with their world and make ourselves irrelevant as just another adult who "doesn't get it."

Yes, the reality is that the Internet can be an extremely dangerous playground for kids. No, we cannot afford to alienate ourselves from our kids' circle of trust, because they really, really need our help to navigate the online world safely. Through Activity 14, we start from a place of common ground—the idea that technology can be fun—and thereby put ourselves in a great position to dialogue openly with kids about technology in general: the good, the bad, and of course, the ugly.

And while you may, at times, feel like a visitor in your child's digital world, keep in mind that any lack of technological expertise on your part is made up for by your more sophisticated social and moral insights. In short; *when it comes to understanding 21st-century technology, you need your kids and your kids need you.* Do everything you can to make sure you stick together!

TIPS TO HELP KIDS UNDERSTAND THE ACTIVITY

- Encourage kids to talk to you about their responses to the nine thought questions in their *Activity Book.* Use open-ended questions and conversation starters, such as "Tell me more about . . ." and "Help me understand . . . ," to foster elaboration on each topic.
- Do all that you can to listen well and convey genuine interest in what kids are telling you about their online world. While hearing about one more app or video game may feel mind-numbing to you at times, remember that the more you make time to hear about the "little things" in a child's life, the more they will trust you enough to tell you the "big things" when it really matters.
- Give kids the empowering sense that they are knowledgeable when it comes to technology. This will help create an atmosphere of open, nondefensive discussion in which kids feel proud of what they know and eager to share it with you.

- Educate yourself on all that is new in the child/tween/teen worlds of technology. In 8 *Keys to End Bullying: Strategies for Parents & Professionals*, readers are encouraged to consider:
  - ◊ What are the specific challenges, brought on by technology, that today's young people face?
  - ◊ How are they similar to the challenges you faced growing up?
  - ◊ In what ways are they entirely distinct?
  - ◊ How can you help kids overcome the challenges of living in an ever-connected world?
  - ◊ What are the latest social media sites, apps, and venues that kids are using?
  - ◊ How will you become well versed in these latest media so that you can speak knowledgeably about them with kids and intervene effectively when needed?

ACTIVITY 15 5 "Bests" of Technology

In Activity 14, kids are encouraged to think about their favorite app and to write about ways in which the app can potentially impact friendships. In this Activity, kids are challenged to go even deeper in their consideration of the ups and downs of smartphones, apps, social media, the Internet, and gaming by mapping out:

- Five ways that technology helps them to have fun and connect with friends AND
- Five ways that technology can be used to hurt or embarrass people.

To encourage a solution-oriented mindset, Activity 15 challenges young readers to come up with at least one thing they could personally do to counter or fix each of the hurtful online behaviors on their list.

WHAT KIDS LEARN

Summer vacation is awesome—but sometimes it does get too hot. Dessert is the best part of any meal—except when you're already too full. There are good sides and bad sides to everything in life. This is also true of technology. In this activity, you'll focus on the best things about smartphones, social media, the Internet, and gaming. You'll also learn how to turn negatives (such as cyberbullying) into positives.

5 "Bests" of Today's Technology

A. Make a list of at least 5 ways that technology helps you have fun and connect with others:

1.
2.
3.
4.
5.

B. Now, using the table below, list 5 ways that technology can be used to hurt someone. Write your answer on the left side of the table, under "Hurtful Uses of Technology."

C. Next, for each negative item listed on the left, use the line on the right side of the table to write at least 1 positive thing you could do to make the bad situation better. An example is provided.

HURTFUL USES OF TECHNOLOGY	WAYS TO FIX THE PROBLEM
1. *Example:* Posting an embarrassing photo of someone	1. *Example:* • Take a screen shot and show it to a helpful adult • Delete the photo from my device • Tell the sender to stop • If it's posted on social media, use the app's anonymous reporting system
2.	2.
3.	3.
4.	4.
5.	5.

KEY POINT

Anytime you turn a negative into a positive in your life, you show that you are responsible and respectful. It's normal for adults who care about you to worry about the dangers of cyberbullying. These adults are showing that they care for you when they limit your use of gadgets. Every time you turn what could be a problem into a smart solution, you earn an adult's trust. You also show them you are mature enough to enjoy all the great things technology offers.

WHAT ADULTS NEED TO KNOW

It's helpful when parents, teachers, counselors, and other helping adults make a concerted effort to view technology through the exciting, positive lens that most kids use and to avoid dwelling on the downsides of smartphones, video games, apps, and social media. As discussed in the previous activity, a prevailing negative mindset about kids' use of technology too often results in barriers to open and honest adult–child communication.

A great alternative to overfocusing on the risks of gadgets and devices is helping kids conduct their own realistic analysis of the problems posed by common uses of technology alongside practical ways to fix each problem. Encouraging this kind of solution focus in young people has benefits that extend far beyond helping them plan to overcome technology's glitches.

TIPS TO HELP KIDS UNDERSTAND THE ACTIVITY

- Encourage kids to talk about five ways that today's technology helps them to have fun and connect with others.

◊ Are there any items on this list that are especially important to your child?

◊ Is there anything you can do to facilitate greater enjoyment of your child's gadgets or better online connections with peers?

- Looking at your child's 5 "Bests" list, do you have any specific concerns? For example, are their activities that your child enjoys but that you find potentially risky or unacceptable?

  ◊ How can you address this discrepancy in a way that will bring you and your child together as problem-solvers?

  ◊ Is there room for flexibility or compromise on your part? By your child?

- Encourage kids to share their analysis of Hurtful Uses of Technology vs. Ways to Fix the Problem:

  ◊ Which problems seem to have ready solutions?

  ◊ Are there problems that pose too big a challenge for kids to be able to fix? If so, help kids brainstorm realistic things they can do to improve a problem situation, even if they can't fix it entirely.

- Ask kids to comment on:

  ◊ Which problem on the Hurtful Uses list occurs most often?

  ◊ Which problem is the hardest to deal with?

  ◊ Which problem(s) can you handle on your own? Which require the help of an adult?

  ◊ Who can you go to for help in addressing online cruelty and cyberbullying?

  ◊ What happens to kids when they try to stop cyberbullying? Do things usually get better? What could make a cyberbullying situation worse?

    - NOTE: It is important to directly acknowledge and address the fears that young people have about intervening to stop bullying.

    - Talking about how to overcome real-world challenges is extremely empowering to kids. Young people don't want to hear unrealistic or quick fixes from adults; they need a detailed road map of what to do—along with Plan B and Plan C if their original "fix" fails.

ACTIVITY 16 Rules of Netiquette

You're familiar with the saying "What happens in Vegas . . . ," but did you know that the same thing is true for a young person's online activities? Teaching kids about the far-reaching and indelible mark made by their "digital footprint" is a vital part of online safety as well as a key in preventing online cruelty and cyberbullying.

WHAT KIDS LEARN

In this section, you will find 10 guidelines for using technology—cell phones, texting, apps, social media, computers, tablets, gaming devices, and so on—in ways that are fun for you, safe for your future, and respectful of others.

Put a bookmark in this page of your Activity Book or tear out the Rules of Netiquette and post them somewhere where you can read and review them often.

Rules of Netiquette

RULE 1: Choose Your Words Carefully

If you wouldn't say something to a person's face, don't text it or post it online. Technology makes it too easy to say things that are unkind. Also, the person reading your message can't see the look on your face or hear the tone of your voice. Trying to be sarcastic or funny doesn't always come across online. *Type carefully as well.* Don't use ALL CAPS, since they make it look as if you are angry or YELLING. #dontsaydontsend

RULE 2: The Internet Is Not a Weapon

Don't gossip about other people through texts or online. It's not okay to talk about people behind their backs. Also, social media sites should not be used to leave people out or to "de-friend" a person after a fight.

RULE 3: Who Is This Message For?

Though you may think you are sending a private message or photo to one friend, keep in mind that it can be cut, pasted, and forwarded to an endless number of people. Never post a photo or message that you wouldn't want "everyone" to be able to view.

Be thoughtful about the photos and videos that you allow your friends to take of you. Sometimes, these photos start off as fun, but they can be used in embarrassing ways later on. Always have all of your clothes on in pictures and videos. Seriously.

RULE 4: What You Post Is Permanent

Once you share something online, you lose control of where it goes, who can forward it, who will see it, and how it can be used. You might believe right now that you can trust your best friend with secrets, but you should not send personal information online. You can't imagine it now, but someday, that information could be twisted and used against you.

Commit to a kindness-only policy for your posts. Do not ever use technology to say ugly or mean things about anyone or to anyone. Stop and ask yourself, "What would Mom think if she read this?" Post accordingly.

RULE 5: Take It Slow

The online world can be very fast paced. You may be tempted to say whatever comes to your mind in a given moment. Don't do it! Slow down and think before you post. Wait until you have had a chance to think things through. Cool your head before you post a message that can't be taken back.

RULE 6: Report It

Most social media websites have easy, anonymous reporting systems. Anytime you learn that cyberbullying is taking place, report it right away. The site will take down the content, and you can feel good knowing that you took action to help yourself or another victim of cyberbullying. For most social media sites, the general reporting address is: abuse@websitename.com

RULE 7: Unplug Every Once in a While

A first step in stopping cyberbullying is logging off from an account temporarily. You can instantly end a digital conversation and should plan to do so the minute you recognize that cruelty has begun. In cases where unkindness is repeated, block the person altogether.

RULE 8: Don't Talk to Strangers

Remember that message your parents gave you when you were little? It still applies today and is very important to remember when you are online. Strangers hide in cyberspace and have clever ways of learning about you. Never share private information online, including your full name, home address, personal photos, school name, or phone number.

The same is true for "followers" on social media sites. There is a very, very, VERY big difference between real friends and online followers. Remember that quality of friendships is much more important than quantity. Plan to spend most of your time and energy on your real-life friendships rather than on anonymous cyber-followers.

RULE 9: Set Strong Passwords

Set strong passwords on all of your accounts. Make sure that the only person who is speaking for you is YOU.

RULE 10: It's (NOT!) Nice to Share

For most of your life, you've been told that it's nice to share with others. When it comes to your passwords, though, just DON'T do it! Your accounts are *your* accounts. Don't let any friend—even a best friend—post or text from your account. Ever.

The exception to this rule is your parents. DO share your passwords with them. Don't think of it as invading your privacy. Know that this is the best way for your parents to keep you safe from harm.

WRITE ABOUT IT

Young readers are invited to use the space provided in their Activity Books to add their own commonsense rules for using technology safely and respectfully.

WHAT ADULTS NEED TO KNOW

In *8 Keys to End Bullying: Strategies for Parent & Schools*, I suggest that one of the most important things that caring adults can do to prevent and end cyberbullying is to empower young people to be their own first line of defense (Whitson, 2014). As such, I provide specific, practical, easy-to-implement strategies that kids of any age can use, including advice on:

- Why it's important to reach out to adults and how they can help stop cyberbullying
- The problem with getting revenge online; how to disengage from troubling interactions
- When to log off and block people
- Using privacy settings as a way of setting healthy boundaries
- How to take and use screen shots
- The importance of never forwarding, sharing, or passively condoning cyberbullying in any way
- The critical role bystanders can play in stopping online cruelty and cyberbullying
- How to stop the depersonalization that occurs with online interactions and develop empathy for victims of cyberbullying
- The role of personal accountability in deterring online aggression

Full details on each of these strategies are included in Chapter 4 (Deal Directly With Cyberbullying) of the *8 Keys to End Bullying* book.

TIPS TO HELP KIDS UNDERSTAND THE ACTIVITY

- Make time to review each of the 10 *Rules of Netiquette* with young people. It may make sense to talk about them over the course of several conversations, rather than all at once, to avoid sounding as if you are lecturing. Lessons learned over time are often the most effective.
- Let kids take the lead in explaining each rule to you. Challenge them to talk about things like:
    ◊ What the rule is about
    ◊ Why it matters
    ◊ How it could apply to their everyday life
- Encourage kids to talk about a real-life situation in which:
    ◊ One (or more) of the rules was broken, and what the results were
    ◊ One (or more) of the rules was followed, and how a situation improved
- Is there a rule on the list that your child finds especially important? Which one? Why?
- Is there any rule that your child disagrees with? Which one? How could the rule be adjusted to make it more effective in their life?
- Challenge kids to think about Rule 7: Unplug Every Once in a While. Ask them to think about how long they could remain "unplugged" from their peers and to talk about what they think they would miss out on while they were offline.
- Encourage kids to dialogue with you about their thoughts on privacy and what it means to them to share their online activities with parents or other caring adults.
- In "Write About It," kids are encouraged to write down their own common-sense rules of netiquette. Encourage kids to share their ideas with you and talk about the real-world applications of their suggested rules.

ACTIVITY 17 To Send or Not to Send?

One "Rule of Netiquette" that has received significant attention in the media, among software developers, and even from young entrepreneurs is the idea of *taking it slow* and pausing before posting content online and via text. In late 2015, Apple partnered with the I Am a Witness campaign to release a new emoji specifically designed to call attention to cyberbullying. The idea behind the picture of an eye inside a speech bubble is that when someone witnesses online cruelty, they can send or post the emoji to label the content as cyberbullying and to show support to its target (Burke, 2015).

Another popular app, called ReThink (Rutherford-Morrison, 2015), was created by a then 13-year-old girl who was inspired to action after the cyberbullying-related suicide of an 11-year-old girl from Florida. Creator Trisha Prabhu was named a global finalist in Google's 2014 Science Fair for this app, which uses pop-up messages to alert users if a post they are about to send is potentially offensive. ReThink asks people to pause before they post and ask themselves, "This message may be hurtful to others. Would you like to pause, review and rethink before posting?" To learn more, please visit www.rethinkwords.com.

Activity 17 helps kids teach kids the importance of thinking before they post. Featuring typical texts, posts, and emails, young readers are challenged to consider the appropriateness of each digital message and make a thoughtful decision as to whether or not it should be sent.

WHAT KIDS LEARN:

Following a brief, fun, creative activity in which readers get to design their own smartphone case and customized home screen, kids complete this activity:

To Send or Not to Send? is a follow-up to Activity 16, in which you learned the Rules of Netiquette. Now, you'll put the *Rules* to work!

Directions:

- First, use the space below to design your own smartphone case and home screen.
- Then, read real-life texts, emails, and posts from other people's phones. Decide whether or not they should be sent.

_____**'s Smartphone**
[FILL IN YOUR NAME HERE]

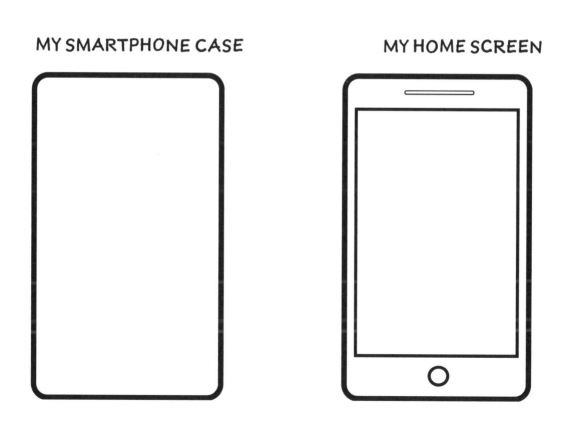

MY SMARTPHONE CASE

MY HOME SCREEN

To Send or Not to Send?

Directions:

Beneath each smartphone screen, circle the word SEND if you think the message follows the Rules of Netiquette. Circle DELETE if you think the message would hurt a friendship or someone's feelings.

PHONE 1:

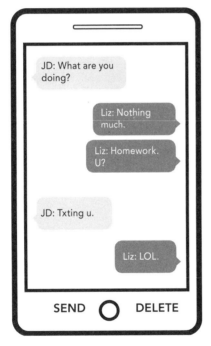

> JD: What are you doing?
>
> Liz: Nothing much.
>
> Liz: Homework. U?
>
> JD: Txting u.
>
> Liz: LOL.

SEND ◯ DELETE

PHONE 2:

> Best. Party. Ever. Don't you wish you were invited?

SEND ◯ DELETE

PHONE 3:

@LucyLC I deleted u and unfollowed u. No one likes u and u r going 2 b alone ur whole life.

SEND DELETE

PHONE 4

Hey—
Do you want to go to the movies on Friday, then sleepover? Emily and Aimee are coming too. Lmk.

SEND ◯ DELETE

PHONE 5

Kateeeee: i have to tell you something but promise not to tell?

HannahBanana: promise.

Kateeeee: jesse is going to ask out kaylee but i know for a fact that kaylee does not like him.

HannahBanana: ouch.

Kateeeee: yup. I want 2 b there to see his face.

HannahBanana: can u say PUBLIC REJECTION.

SEND ◯ DELETE

PHONE 6

Mayamaya: Still coming over to hang out?

LMZ3: omg. totally forgot! made other plans.

Mayamaya: Seriously?

LMZ3: so sorry! I'll totally make it up to you!

Mayamaya: No way. You ruined my whole night. I could have gone to Stacy's house but I told her I was hanging out with you. I hate you.

SEND DELETE

WHAT ADULTS NEED TO KNOW

Impulsivity is a hallmark of child and adolescent behavior. Caught up in their own intense emotions or simply swept up in their very 21st-century world of constant contact and instant communication, kids often say what they feel in the moment—and post it online. And yet, blurting out whatever thought or feeling comes to their mind is not inevitable. Kids can be taught the skill of carefully considering their words before ever speaking them or posting them online.

Research on the ReThink app created by teen developer Trisha Prabhu shows that adolescents changed their mind a whopping 93% of the time and made the decision not to post offensive and cruel messages on social media, based on the app's simple reminder to think before posting hurtful content (ReThink, 2015). This is incredibly encouraging news, especially for parents and educators who play the critical role in teaching kids to *take it slow*.

Another tool utilized by many helping adults is the technology contract. In the *8 Keys to End Bullying* book, these contracts are described in depth. While this kind of agreement, mutually developed by adults and kids through conversations and exchanges of ideas, are not legally binding documents that prevent any online mistakes or misbehavior from ever occurring (don't we all wish?), they are a great way to clearly define technology usage guidelines and have kids commit to using technology safely and respectfully. When technology contracts are revisited and referred to on a regular basis (read: not put on a shelf or filed away, never to be discussed again), they are especially helpful in getting kids to think about whether or not to post specific content.

A sample technology contract that can be used or adapted for your specific needs can be found at the end of this Activity.

TIPS TO HELP KIDS UNDERSTAND THE ACTIVITY

- The design-your-own-smartphone-case-and-home-screen activity is designed as a creative, right-brained activity as well as a springboard for discussion about texting, messaging, and posting spontaneous thoughts and feelings. Start by encouraging kids to share their designs with you, then move the discussion into the more in-depth questions featured below:
    - ◊ How do you know whether or not a message is "appropriate" to send online? What are the rules you use to guide your personal decisions?
    - ◊ Tell about a time when you or someone you know was hurt by an online text or post.
        - Has there ever been a time in your life when personal information about you was sent online without permission?
        - What happened?
        - How did this incident make you feel?
        - How did it affect your friendships?
    - ◊ Did any of the examples in the Activity sound familiar to you? If so, which ones? What happened in your situation?
- Consider developing your own technology contract with your child or a group of children with whom you are working based on the guidelines noted above.

Sample Technology Contract

I, _____ understand that my access to a smartphone, email, computer, video games, social media, and other forms of technology is a privilege that comes with rules. These rules are based on our family's values and beliefs.

1. The device(s) I am using belong to my parents. They have the right to take my access away if I am not following the rules of this contract.

2. All of my online activities can and may be viewed by my parents at any time. My parents will always be informed about any apps I download and accounts I create.

3. I will set strong passwords and tell my parents the passwords I create for every account. I will not share my passwords with friends.

4. I will always be kind online. I will never use technology to say ugly, nasty, or mean things about anyone. I will not tease, spread gossip about, hurt, or deceive others with technology. I will never post a photo of someone else without their permission.

5. I know that what happens online stays online, so I will always use my best judgment in what I say and post. I will not let others post potentially embarrassing or reputation-damaging photos of me. I will neither send pictures of my private parts nor receive photos of anyone else's private parts.

6. I will take it slow and think before I post anything, especially if I am feeling angry or upset.

7. I will put my phone in the charger promptly at 9:00pm every school night and every weekend night at 10:00pm. I will not use it again until at least 7:00am.

8. I can bring my cell phone to school, but it will stay locked in my locker throughout the school day.

9. When I am in public or even in the company of friends and family, I will not use my device. I will always give priority to person-to-person communication and face-to-face conversations.

10. I know that it's okay to be bored sometimes and that not having anything to do for a while gives me time to have creative, original thoughts. Therefore, I will make sure to wonder about things without googling them right away, stand in a line and purposely take notice of the world around me instead of immediately getting my phone out, look out the window when I am a passenger in a car, and keep my eyes looking forward as often as I can.

11. If I am ever the target of online cruelty or I learn that cyberbullying is taking place, I will report it right away.

12. If I ever get an email, text, or friend/follower request from someone I don't personally know, I will delete it and block the person if necessary.

13. I will not open attachments or click on links unless I know exactly what they are and feel certain that they were sent by a safe source. If I ever have any doubt about the sender or the link, I will get approval from my parents before opening it.

14. I understand that predators and scammers lurk in cyberspace. I will never post or send personally identifying information online, including my address, phone number, age, birthdate, school, password, or social security number.

15. I will never (ever!) ignore a text or phone call if the screen reads "Mom" or "Dad."

16. If my device breaks, I am responsible for the costs of replacing or repairing it.

17. These rules are subject to change as I get older and as new apps and social media websites are developed.

Signed: _____

Date: _____

Parent Signature(s): _____

To Send or Not to Send?

ANSWER KEY

Phone 1: SEND

This is a fun text between friends. It can be sent with no worries.

Phone 2: DELETE

Social media should never be used to hurt someone or make them feel excluded on purpose. This post seems to have no purpose other than to make the other person feel left out. It should be deleted.

Phone 3: DELETE

The Internet is not a weapon. Never send a message with hateful, cruel words—even if you are really, really mad at someone. Delete a post like this before the way you're feeling now turns into permanent cruelty.

Phone 4: SEND

Email is a great way to send brief messages and make plans with friends. This email can be sent!

Phone 5: DELETE

Don't use your phone to gossip, spread rumors, or take joy in someone else's pain. These texts just show how low Kateeeee and HannahBanana can go. They should be deleted before ever being sent.

Phone 6: DELETE

Mayamaya may have a right to be angry, but she does not have a right to text (or speak!) to LMZ3 that way. She should delete this text before her friendship is ruined for good.

ACTIVITY 18 When Your Message Gets Mixed Up Online

Have you ever read a text, post, message, or email from a friend, relative, co-worker, or boss and felt totally insulted by it? You weren't able to get over how rude or thoughtless the person was until you ran into him or her and heard them speak the same words out loud, only to realize that they were just trying to be funny? Or that the snarky tone you thought you heard was really just that person's trademark sarcasm?

For both adults and kids, meaning can very easily become lost in translation online. This Activity is designed to help young people explore how online communication differs from face-to-face speech and learn strategies to confirm the meaning of any hard-to-interpret online messages.

WHAT KIDS LEARN

In Activity 11, you learned about *Mean*, *Meek*, and *Mean-It* responses. Then, in Activity 12, you learned about how tone of voice changes the meaning of your messages. But what happens when you say something in a text or online and there is no tone of voice to go with it? If there are no *Mean*, *Meek*, and *Mean-It* tones online, how can you know what a person is truly saying to you—and how to best respond?

Directions:
For this activity, you will need red, yellow, and green pencils or crayons.

PART I: READ THE SITUATION BELOW.

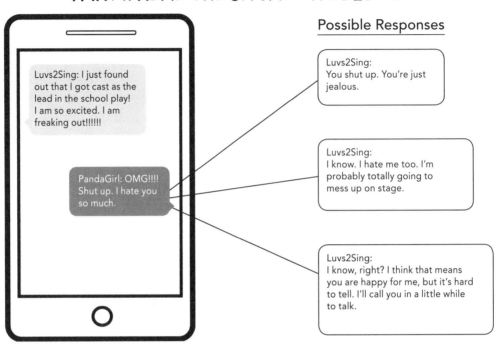

Possible Responses

Luvs2Sing: I just found out that I got cast as the lead in the school play! I am so excited. I am freaking out!!!!!!

PandaGirl: OMG!!!! Shut up. I hate you so much.

Luvs2Sing:
You shut up. You're just jealous.

Luvs2Sing:
I know. I hate me too. I'm probably totally going to mess up on stage.

Luvs2Sing:
I know, right? I think that means you are happy for me, but it's hard to tell. I'll call you in a little while to talk.

PART 2: USING YOUR COLORED PENCILS OR CRAYONS, SHADE EACH RESPONSE ABOVE AS FOLLOWS:

- The first response is **Mean**. It would insult PandaGirl and make the situation worse. Color it RED.
- The second response is **Meek**. Luvs2Sing takes PandaGirl's text literally and responds by downplaying her good news. Color it YELLOW.
- The third response is a **Mean-It** one. This text is honest and direct without being

mean or meek. Talking to someone in person is the best way to clear up any confusing online messages. Color it GREEN.

PART 3: IN THE SPACE BELOW, WRITE IN YOUR OWN POSSIBLE MEAN, MEEK, AND MEAN-IT RESPONSES TO THE TEXT CONVERSATION.

- Color the **Mean** response red, the **Meek** response yellow, and the **Mean-It** response green.
- Whenever you respond to an unclear text or online post, make sure that the only response you give a GREEN light to is a *Mean-It* one. #thinkbeforeyoupost

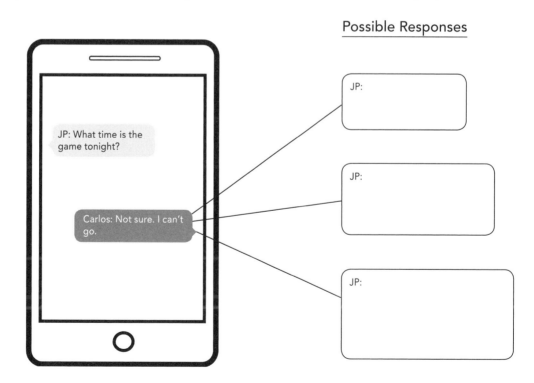

Possible Responses

JP:

JP:

JP:

JP: What time is the game tonight?

Carlos: Not sure. I can't go.

MORE TO THINK ABOUT

The questions below will help you to think more about how meaning can sometimes get confused through texts and online. Talk about this with a parent, relative, teacher, counselor, or other trustworthy adult. You can use the lines provided to jot down thoughts about each question.

1.   How is talking online different from talking face-to-face?

_____

_____

_____

2.   How could a text, post, photo, or online message be misunderstood by a reader? Give an example from your own life.

_____

_____

3.   Do you think it is easier for someone to be cruel online than it is for them to be cruel in person?

_____

4.   Has there ever been a time when you misunderstood someone's online post? Did you think they were being mean when really they were trying to be funny?

_____

_____

5.   Have you ever returned a cruel text with an ever crueler one? What happened?

_____

_____

WHAT ADULTS NEED TO KNOW

If you have ever had the experience of misinterpreting someone's typed or texted words, you know firsthand how confusing and painful this can be. For young people who may easily get swept away by emotion and assumption or have a harder time taking someone else's perspective (more on developing this skill in Activity 28), misconstruing text (and subtext) can take a lasting toll on friendships. Caring adults can play a very helpful role with this issue by:

1. Helping kids to consider various interpretations of online messages. Simply reading messages aloud to kids can help them consider an alternate meaning. Also, challenging kids to think through "the facts" of their relationship with the sender is also valuable: "Is it typical for this person to say mean things to you? Does this friend have a reason to be angry with you?"

2. If you and the child can reasonably assume that the answer to these questions is "no," help the child craft a response that is neither defensive nor offensive but seeks to check on the person's meaning. For instance, in the example where PandaGirl says, "OMG!!!! Shut up. I hate you so much," an effective fact-checker response could be, "I know, right? I think that means you are happy for me, but it's hard to tell. I'll call you in a little while to talk."

3. On the other hand, if a child reaches out to you for help in interpreting an online message and you reasonably conclude that the message is cruel, you have an important moment on your hands:

   - Use the opportunity to empathize with the pain and confusion the child is feeling. A hug, silent moments of solidarity, and something as simple as saying, "I'm sorry this was said to you. You don't deserve to be treated like this," can go a very long way.
   - Teach the child specific skills for disengaging from the emotionally charged interaction with the peer by logging off from the conversation,

blocking the peer if this is a pattern of behavior or if the message is especially cruel, and/or taking a screen shot of the message if need be. For abusive posts online, you may need to consider showing the child how to report the content to the proper monitors.

TIPS TO HELP KIDS UNDERSTAND THE ACTIVITY

- Encourage kids to share real-life experiences they have had with struggling to interpret online messages.
- If you are leading this activity with a group of young people, try to create an atmosphere where kids feel safe to have a genuine back-and-forth dialogue with each other and to discover how common of an experience it is to receive questionable messages online and to struggle with how to interpret them.
- Ask kids to consider the merits of disengaging from cruel online messages. In this world of instant replies and constant contact, kids sometimes fail to consider that *not* responding at all is a real, powerful, and viable option. Encourage kids to understand that *taking it slow* and waiting to respond—or in some cases choosing not to respond at all—is one of the smartest, best responses they can make.
- Work through Part 3 of the exercise with kids. Help them craft effective responses (even if that means no immediate response) to Carlos's text. Challenge kids to weigh the pros and cons of various response options and to predict the likely outcome of each on the relationship between Carlos and JP.

ACTIVITY 19 The Student Is the Teacher

Young people spend much of their time as students, learning from their teachers. In this Activity, the student *is* the teacher! What better way for kids to learn how to use technology in fun, safe, respectful ways than to teach these principles to other kids?

Activity 19 gives young readers the opportunity to create an informative presentation on stopping online cruelty and cyberbullying that is fun, hands-on, practical, interesting, unforgettable . . . and hopefully brilliant!

WHAT KIDS LEARN

In this Activity, you will create a presentation. It will be fun, hands-on, interesting, informative, and, well, just plain **brilliant**. Plan to wow your audience with a lesson on **Tips for Stopping Cyberbullying**. Let your creative juices flow!

- You can choose to script a one-act play that shows kids standing up to cyberbullying
- You may design a poster with interesting facts and tips to stop online cruelty

Better yet, consider ways that can you use technology to teach about technology!

- Create and share an anti-bullying video message for your peers. With your parent's permission, upload it to YouTube so that it can be viewed by an even wider audience.
- Put together a brief PowerPoint presentation to teach your classmates about cyberbullying.

Whatever format you use, this is your opportunity to make your world a better place by teaching others to use technology respectfully.

Use the Presentation Plan on the next page to map out your presentation.

TIPS FOR STOPPING CYBERBULLYING

Presentation Plan

Format: (circle one)   Video   Play   Poster   Other: _____

Who I will present to: _____

Who I will talk to about scheduling the presentation: _____

Presentation date: _____

Use the following checklist to be sure key ideas are included in your presentation:

☐ Define cyberbullying.

☐ Give examples of common devices that are used to hurt others online.

☐ Explain why cyberbullying is a problem for young people.

☐ List at least 5 things kids can do to use technology respectfully.

☐ List at least 5 things kids can do to deal with cyberbullying when they become aware of it.

☐ Give an example of something kind a kid could say to someone else who has been cyberbullied.

Presentation Planning Notes:

_____

_____

_____

_____

_____

_____

_____

_____

_____

WHAT ADULTS NEED TO KNOW

One of the best ways to educate young people about the rewards and risks of technology is by encouraging them to share helpful information with each other. This approach acknowledges that kids are the true experts when it comes to online interactions and empowers them to use their expertise in helpful (rather than hurtful) ways.

Adults can play an especially supportive role with this Activity by helping kids gather necessary supplies, such as poster board and markers, and facilitating access to technology so that kids can do research online, make a video, and/or create a PowerPoint presentation.

TIPS TO HELP KIDS UNDERSTAND THE ACTIVITY

- Encourage kids to use technology to teach about technology. A presentation that includes PowerPoint or a video is especially helpful because it engages young people directly with their subject matter and shows them firsthand the fun, constructive uses of technology—in stark contrast to the destructive uses advised against in the presentation they develop.
- Be an encouraging, interested audience member.
- Give genuine, positive feedback on the presentation.
- Ask smart, challenging (not interrogating!) questions about what kids present.
- Use the kids' content as a springboard for discussion. In particular, after the presentation, engage kids in a conversation about the five practical ways they suggest that kids use technology respectfully and the five realistic things young people can do to stop cyberbullying.
- If you are working with a group of kids, consider having them work in small groups of three to four to prepare their presentations. Host an event in which multiple presentations are shared for younger audience members as well as for parents.
- Research various opportunities for kids to submit their presentations to local or national bullying prevention campaigns. Several organizations sponsor annual contests for kid-generated videos, posters, and presentations.

ACTIVITY 20 Pledge to Be Cyberbullying Free

Activities 14 through 19 give tech-savvy young people the opportunity to consider many of the fun ways to use technology safely and respectfully as well as over a dozen practical strategies for stopping online cruelty and cyberbullying. In the final Activity of this section, kids are asked to put all of their new knowledge and skills together.

WHAT KIDS LEARN

A *pledge* is a way to say that you will follow certain rules or guidelines. On the next page, you'll find a pledge. It asks you to promise that when you use technology, you will be honorable, responsible, and kind. Read through each statement in the pledge. Consider how your use of smartphones, tablets, computers, video games, and other devices can change or improve, based on these rules. <u>Are you ready to do your part to make technology a safe, fun way for kids to connect?</u>

This pledge can be signed and kept inside this Activity Book. Or, you may carefully tear it out and place it somewhere you'll see it often. That way, the guidelines will stay fresh in your mind. Perhaps a class at school—or your entire school—will want to make a similar pledge. Ask a trustworthy teacher to share the pledge with a group of kids. You can all work together to keep online interactions respectful and fun.

I PLEDGE TO BE CYBERBULLYING FREE

1. I will text, share, and post only items that I consider kind and would be willing to say to someone in person.

2. I will always take time to think before I post my thoughts, responses, or photos, especially if I'm feeling angry or sad.

3. If I see cyberbullying, I will do whatever I can to stop it. I will not join in. I will not just ignore it. I know how to report cyberbullying and who to report it to.

4. I will use strong passwords and protect others' rights to privacy.

5. I will balance my time between online interactions and face-to-face friendships.

6. I will enjoy what technology has to offer in safe, respectful, kind ways at all times.

ADD YOUR OWN PROMISES HERE:

7. _____

_____

8. _____

_____

Signed: _____

Date: _____

Witness: _____

MORE TO THINK ABOUT

1. This pledge left you 2 open spaces to write in your own commitments to safe, respectful online interactions. If you had even more spaces, what would you have added?

_____

_____

2. Are there any commitments on the pledge that seem difficult to you? Which one(s)?

_____

_____

3. Who did you choose as your "Witness" to sign the pledge?

_____

- The purpose of having a Witness is to connect you with someone—maybe a friend, a family member, or a teacher—who can help you keep your pledge. That person can tell you if you have crossed a line into online cruelty or cyberbullying.

- All of us need a person in our lives who is honest enough to tell us when we have messed up and wise enough to help us make things right again.

WHAT ADULTS NEED TO KNOW

There is so much that adults can do to support kids in their efforts to enjoy the fun aspects of technology while avoiding its pitfalls. On the next page, you'll find a pledge that you, as a parent, professional, or adult who cares about the safety and emotional well-being of young people, can make, committing your time, your effort, your knowledge, and your support to kids as they grow up in an ever-connected world:

I Pledge to Help Kids Stay CYBERBULLYING FREE

1. I will do all that I can to listen well and convey genuine interest in what kids are telling me about their online world.

2. I will empower young people by teaching them specific, practical, easy-to-implement strategies to stop online cruelty and cyberbullying.

3. I will keep myself up-to-date on the latest apps, social media networks, online lingo, video games, devices, and other developments in the technology used most often by kids.

4. I will role-model the Rules of Netiquette. I will think before I post and never use technology to be unkind in any way. I will demonstrate for young people how to balance my time between online interactions and face-to-face relationships.

5. **If I become aware of cyberbullying, I will do whatever I can to stop it. If a young person reports online cruelty or cyberbullying to me, I will take the report seriously and do all that I can to make the situation better.**

6. I will use a technology contract with my own child and/or kids with whom I work and revisit it often to make sure that we are both maintaining our commitments.

7. I will be a supportive resource for kids in helping them consider various interpretations of online messages and understand the important differences between online and face-to-face interactions.

Signed: _____

Date: _____

Witness: _____

TIPS TO HELP KIDS UNDERSTAND THE ACTIVITY

- Talk with kids about the *I Pledge to Be Cyberbullying Free* pledge. Ask them if they think all of the most important rules for using technology safely and respectfully are covered.
- The pledge leaves young people two open spaces to write in their own commitments to safe, respectful online interactions. Encourage kids to share with you the two additional commitments they wrote. If the child did not fill in the extra spaces, challenge them to do so by asking them about the most important lesson or skill they learned from this section of the *Activity Book.*
- Ask kids: Are there any commitments on the pledge that seem difficult to you? If so, which one(s)? Who can you go to for help in fulfilling that commitment?
- Encourage kids to tell you about the person they chose as their "Witness" to sign the pledge.
  - ◊ Let kids know that the purpose of having a Witness is to connect them with at least one person who is willing to help them stay committed to safe, respectful online behavior and to hold them accountable if they ever cross a line into online cruelty or cyberbullying.
  - ◊ Reassure young people that all of us (even adults!) need a person in our lives who is honest enough to tell us when we have messed up and wise enough to help us make things right again.
  - ◊ If the child did not choose a Witness or can't think of someone they would ask, offer to fill this role for them. This is a powerful way to reach out to kids and convey your support. At the same time, becoming aware of a young person's belief that they have no one to witness their pledge or support them in stopping cyberbullying is important information; this is a child who may be lacking caring adult connections and may benefit greatly from your help in cultivating them.

- If you are using the 8 *Keys Activity Book* with a group of kids, consider having all of them sign the pledge at the same time and perhaps hang them in a common, high-traffic area. Kids may enjoy taking turns reading the pledge statements aloud or talking about practical ways to live out each guideline. Creating a sense that all of the kids are working together to keep online interactions respectful and fun can be a very powerful commitment and bonding experience.

Level-Up Your Skills to Handle Bullying

ACTIVITY 21 This Is My Brain on Bullying

The human brain is uniquely designed to handle stressful situations such as bullying. All of us are born with both an "emotional" and a "logical" part of our brain that, together, provide us with the ability to choose our responses to any event. In this activity, kids get a mini-lesson in neuroscience and learn how their amazing brain gives them the power to make positive choices whenever they encounter bullying. *Companion Guide* readers will learn how to support this "science lesson" for kids through a supplemental video and a fun, sensory activity.

WHAT KIDS LEARN

Make a fist* with your hand. Now, fold your thumb into your palm and bend your fingers over it. Believe it or not, this is a pretty close model of your brain! In this activity, we will talk about 3 parts of your amazing brain:

1. Your wrist is like the **brain stem**—the part of your brain that connects to your spinal cord. (Your arm is like the spinal cord.) The brain stem controls things that keep you alive, such as your heart rate and breathing.

— Brainstem

* The hand model of the brain is adapted from Siegel, D. (2012). Dr. Daniel Siegel presenting a hand model of the brain [Video file]. Retrieved from https://www.youtube.com/watch?v=gm9CIJ74Oxw

2. Your thumb is like the **limbic system**—the part of your brain that helps you feel your feelings. That is why it is often called your "emotional brain." When you feel sudden anger or sadness after being bullied, your limbic system is working!

Limbic system

KEY POINT: FIGHT, FLIGHT, OR FREEZE

Together, the brain stem and limbic system control your body's *fight, flight, or freeze response*. This is how your body handles stress, no matter what caused it. It happens whether a shark is about to bite you with his teeth or a classmate is about to bully you with his words. For example:

- When someone says something cruel, you might *freeze* up and not know what to do or say.
- When a classmate hits you, you might *fight* back without even thinking.
- When your friends leave you out, you might run away from the room. Another way to say "run away" is *flight*.

These sudden responses mean that your brain stem and limbic system have taken charge of your body!

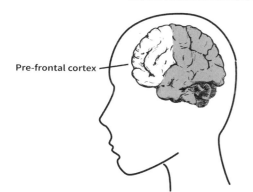

Pre-frontal cortex

3. The front part of your fingers, when wrapped over your thumb, are like the **pre-frontal cortex.** This part of your brain helps you make good decisions. It is also known as your **"logical brain"** because it lets you stop and think before doing what your brain stem and limbic system tell you to do.

This is very important. When bullying happens, you can THINK about your choices for how to respond. Then you can CHOOSE the best decision. Even in bad situations, you can make something good happen.

The Brain Stem, Limbic System, and Pre-frontal Cortex

HERE IS A DIAGRAM OF THE HUMAN BRAIN. It shows the brain stem, limbic system, and pre-frontal cortex. Using the information you have just read, complete the following activity.

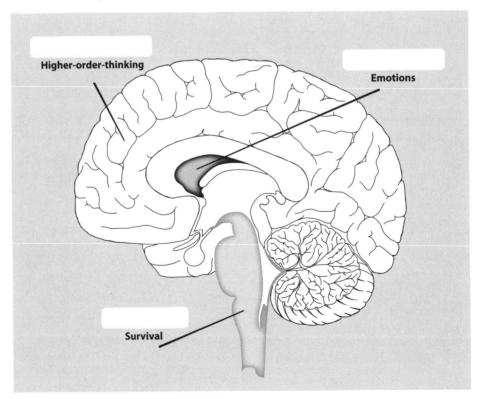

1. In the boxes provided, label the **brain stem**, **limbic system**, and **pre-frontal cortex**.

2. Draw a line to match each part of the brain with what it does:

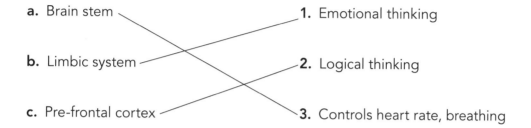

   a. Brain stem   **1.** Emotional thinking

   b. Limbic system   **2.** Logical thinking

   c. Pre-frontal cortex   **3.** Controls heart rate, breathing

3. Lightly shade each section of the brain as follows:
   - Brain stem = blue
   - Limbic system = red
   - Pre-frontal cortex = green

MORE TO THINK ABOUT

What does all of this brain science have to do with bullying?
Whenever someone is cruel to you, your brain is active!

- Your face might get red and feel hot. This is because of what's going on in your brain stem.
- You may feel angry, embarrassed, or sad. This is because of what's going on in your limbic system.

These parts of your brain, when left on their own, may cause you to hit, cry, yell, or do something else that is not nice. It might feel good at the time, but it will make your problem worse.

- On the other hand, if you STOP and think when you notice bullying, you allow your pre-frontal cortex to take control of the other parts of your brain. In doing so, you gain a very important power—*the ability to THINK through your choices and choose the best response.*

In Activity 13, you learned that you always have choices about how to respond to conflict and bullying. **Your pre-frontal cortex is the part of your brain that gives you the ability to choose helpful responses**.

In the next Activity, you will read real-life bullying scenes. Then you will decide if the response to the scene is caused by "emotional brain" reacting or "logical brain" responding.

WHAT ADULTS NEED TO KNOW

The hand model of the brain, shared with young readers in their *Activity Book*, is adapted from Daniel Siegel's Brain Hand Model. For more information and to enhance your understanding of how the human brain responds to stressful incidents, check out Siegel's brief YouTube video (2012), "Dr. Daniel Siegel Presenting a Hand Model of the Brain." This video can be shared with young people as well to supplement the learning from their *Activity Book*.

In terms of development, young people are dominated by their limbic system, or emotional brain (Siegel & Bryson, 2011). Sometimes, they can use their logical brain and sometimes they cannot—especially during periods of stress. Just knowing this is critical because it helps us, as the adults who live, work, and cope with kids' meltdowns, to adjust our expectations and to accept that young people are doing the very best they can with the brain they have.

Insight is a powerful tool for young people. In the YouTube video referenced above, Siegel explains that when kids can "name it, they can tame it," meaning that when we give kids knowledge of their brain's role in coping with stressful situations such as bullying, we empower them to use their logical brain to make the best choices possible in a given situation.

TIPS TO HELP KIDS UNDERSTAND THE ACTIVITY

- Encourage kids to describe each part of the brain—the brain stem, limbic system, and neocortex—in their own words. Check for comprehension and supplement any important details that young readers forget or omit, especially as they relate to how the brain copes with a stressful situation such as bullying.
  - ◊ Review the pages of the *Activity Book* to ensure that the diagram of the brain is labeled and shaded correctly and that the three brain parts are matched with their correct function.
  - ◊ Kids should know that this is not an "academic" exercise with scores for correct vs. incorrect responses, but rather a thought activity intended to help them understand how their amazing brain gives them the power to make good choices in any situation.
- Ask kids to talk about a stressful incident from their own life (it can be about bullying, but it doesn't have to be) and to trace how each of the three parts of their brain were active throughout that incident.
- Describe a stressful incident from your life and share with kids the role that each of the three parts of your brain played in helping you cope.

BONUS ACTIVITY FOR *COMPANION GUIDE* READERS TO SHARE WITH KIDS

- Kids benefit from hands-on, sensory experiences to supplement their learning—particularly with a complex subject such as the one presented in this Activity. This hands-on "sculpting" activity will boost kids' understanding of the brain and add to their fun—making the concepts more memorable in the long term.

- First, simply gather two small handfuls of play dough, preferably in two different colors. I typically use blue and red for good contrast.
- Give the young person the first color and challenge him or her to simply roll the dough in their hands to create a ball.
- Tell the child that this ball of dough represents their emotional brain.
- Remind them of the various feelings processed by their emotional brain during an incident of bullying—such as anger, sadness, fear, humiliation, and loneliness.
- Talk about the fight, flight, or freeze response that is controlled by the emotional brain.
- Next, give the young person the second color of dough to play with for a few minutes. Then, ask them to sculpt the dough so that it covers the top and sides of the first ball of dough.
- Use the diagram of the brain from the Activity Book to give kids a visual guide of how their "brain sculpture" should look when the second color is added.
    ◊ Explain to kids that the second color of dough represents their logical brain. Challenge young people to talk about the functions of their logical brain, with the goal of highlighting that good decision-making is made possible by this part of their brain.
    ◊ Show kids in a very literal way how the logical brain "covers" the emotional brain as a way of protecting it from impulsive, un-thought-out decisions.
    ◊ Encourage kids to add their own comments, thoughts, and observations about the structure of the brain and its role in helping them cope with stressful situations such as bullying.
- Encourage kids to let their dough sculptures harden so that they have a lasting visual reminder of how their amazing brain can help them make good decisions during bullying situations.

ACTIVITY 22 Which Brain Are You Using?

In Activity 21, kids learned about the three parts of their brain involved in responding to stressful situations such as bullying. Most importantly, they learned that their *neocortex* gives them the power to make positive choices whenever they encounter bullying behavior. In Activity 22, kids are presented with five real-life situations and challenged to figure out if they were handled with "emotional brain thinking" or "logical brain thinking."

WHAT KIDS LEARN

Anytime you need to remember how your amazing brain works, just make a fist! Your wrist, thumb, and 4 folded fingers can show you the most important parts of your brain's response to bullying and stress. To review:

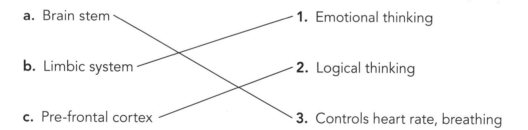

a. Brain stem   1. Emotional thinking

b. Limbic system   2. Logical thinking

c. Pre-frontal cortex   3. Controls heart rate, breathing

WHICH BRAIN?

Directions:

Read each of the situations below. Decide if the response to it is an emotional, limbic system reaction or a thoughtful response by the pre-frontal cortex.

Situation 1:

Mrs. Wagner is handing back the math tests from last week. Kristy gets hers and sees that she made many mistakes. She scored a 5/10 on her test and is very upset. Emily leans over Kristy's desk and yells, "Whadya get? Whadya get?" Kristy is so embarrassed that she yells, "Go away, Emily! It's none of your stupid business!"

Circle which part of her brain Kristy is using to respond to Emily:

Limbic system   Pre-frontal cortex

Situation 2:

Grace and Connor are chosen by the gym teacher to be team captains for kickball. Silas is excited because Connor is his best friend and he thinks Connor will pick him first. Connor doesn't pick Silas first, however. Neither does Grace. In fact, Silas is the very last kid in the whole 3rd grade to be picked for kickball. He is embarrassed and wants to hide. As he walks toward the field with his team, Silas takes a deep breath. He says to himself, "You're going to go out there and play the best game of your life so that next time, you'll be picked first."

Circle which part of his brain Silas is using to respond to being chosen last:

Limbic system   Pre-frontal cortex

Situation 3:

On the bus ride to school, Pete and Cooper make fun of Dawson for wearing his big brother's old clothes. They taunt him for not having the new, name-brand sports gear that Pete and Cooper wear. Dawson looks at his 2 classmates like they are crazy. He says, "Whatever, dudes." Then he turns to the kid on his left and starts a conversation about football.

Circle which part of his brain Dawson is using to respond to being teased:

Limbic system   Pre-frontal cortex

Situation 4:

Every time Charlotte plays with Kayla, Lucy tells her, "Why are you playing with Kayla? You don't even want to be my friend anymore!" Every time Charlotte plays with Lucy, Kayla says, "I won't be your friend anymore if you keep playing with Lucy." Charlotte feels torn because she wants to be friends with *both* girls. The next time Lucy and Kayla ask her to choose sides, Charlotte says in a *Mean-It* voice, "I do want to be your friend. I don't want to fight with you." Then she goes to find a different group of friends to play with at recess.

Circle which part of her brain Charlotte is using to stop this friendship drama:

Limbic system   Pre-frontal cortex

Situation 5:

Gianna and Kessie are texting back and forth one night about Kessie's crush on Lucas. Kessie tells Gianna she is thinking about asking Lucas to the dance. The next day in school, Gianna gets mad at Kessie for not saving her a seat at their lunch table. She takes out her phone, copies the texts where Kessie talks about liking Lucas, and posts them online for their whole 7th-grade class to see.

Circle which part of her brain Gianna is using to get back at Kessie for not saving her a seat:

Limbic system   Pre-frontal cortex

MORE TO THINK ABOUT

In the space below, draw your own comic strip that shows either an *emotional* brain reaction or a *logical* brain response. For added fun, challenge a friend, parent, relative, or teacher to read your cartoon. See if they can tell you which part of the brain is at work.

Circle which part of the brain was used to respond:

Limbic system   Pre-frontal cortex

WHAT ADULTS NEED TO KNOW

Companion Guide readers play a key role in helping young people process each of the scenarios and gain a richer understanding of how their brains function during stressful events such as bullying. The notes below allow you to engage kids in a discussion about the feelings elicited by each situation and the *choices* each character has in responding to them.

Situation 1: Limbic system

Kristy was likely feeling disappointed over her grade and embarrassed to show her score to Emily. In the midst of all of these feelings, Kristy impulsively shoved Emily and spoke to her rudely. Kristy's emotional brain, or limbic system, got the best of her in this situation.

If something like this happens again, Kristy would be much better off pausing to think for a moment, taking a deep breath, and calmly saying to Emily, "Please give me some space, Emily. I don't like to show my grades to other people."

Situation 2: Neocortex

Silas felt humiliated at being picked last and betrayed by his friend, Connor, who he thought would pick him first. Instead of reacting in a negative way, however, he made the choice to breathe deeply and say encouraging words to himself to stay calm.

Situation 3: Neocortex

No one likes to be teased about what they are wearing, but in this situation, instead of showing Pete and Cooper that he was upset by their comments, Dawson chose to keep his cool and act like their teasing didn't bother him one bit. He gave them a nonemotional, two-word response, then turned his focus to kids who were nicer.

Situation 4: Neocortex

It's very difficult to feel caught between different friendships. Charlotte finds herself in a very common situation, in which peers are trying to control who she is (and is not) friends with. Charlotte is too smart and too powerful to let others control her, however. She makes a choice *not to choose* between Lucy and Kayla and responds by finding other friends to play with at recess.

Situation 5: Limbic system

Gianna's feelings are hurt when Kessie does not save her a seat at lunch. Lost in a moment of sadness and anger, she uses her smartphone to try to get back at Kessie by publicly humiliating her.

Next time Gianna gets overwhelmed by her feelings, she should take it slower and pause before posting anything online that could hurt her friend. In a moment of anger, Gianna may have lost a friend permanently.

TIPS TO HELP KIDS UNDERSTAND THE ACTIVITY

- The emphasis in this activity, as in several others throughout the *Activity Book*, is that kids have *choices* in how they respond to bullying and, as such, are *powerful* decision-makers rather than passive victims. Use each situation as a springboard to talk about the positive choices each character has the opportunity to make.
- Share with kids a challenging emotional experience from your childhood or tween years in which you had to make a decision on how to respond.
  ◊ Allow kids to comment on the different possibilities for how you could have responded to the situation.
  ◊ Challenge kids to talk their way through how each different response (positive and negative) would likely have played out.

◊ Tell kids about the choice you made in the situation and the outcome you experienced as a result of your choice.
- Challenge kids to complete the "More to Think About" activity and to share with you their original cartoon.
    ◊ Spend time with the child processing the cartoon.
    ◊ Ask open-ended questions to encourage the child to talk about the scenario in greater detail, including different outcome possibilities.

ACTIVITY 23 Are You a Duck or a Sponge?

In Activities 21 and 22, kids learned about how their amazing brain deals with bullying. The goal of this "Neuroscience 101" for kids is to help them realize that their brain-based responses to bullying play a major role in determining how often—and how severely—the bullying will be repeated. In other words, *kids are powerful!* Using kid-friendly metaphors and a memorable sensory experience, Activity 23 enhances kids' understanding of the power they have to make good choices during any stressful situation.

NOTE: This activity can be completed by kids without the duck and sponge props (noted below), but the metaphor is greatly enhanced when kids can obtain these simple household props and physically carry out the sensory activity. *Companion Guide* readers are urged to help make available the duck, sponge, water, and sink to help bring this memorable demonstration to life.

WHAT KIDS LEARN

For this activity, you will need:

- A rubber duck
- A dry sponge
- 2 cups, both full of water
- A sink

If you don't have these things handy, you will simply need your imagination.

Directions:

1. First, take the dry sponge. Think about how it feels in your hand. Below, circle the word that best describes its weight.

      Heavy   Light

2. Next, hold the sponge in your hand, over the sink. With your other hand, slowly pour one of the cups of water onto the sponge. Try to cover the sponge with the water without spilling it into the sink.

3. Notice how the sponge has changed in response to having water poured over it. Circle the word that best describes its weight now.

      Heavier   Lighter

4. Put the wet sponge aside.

5. Take the rubber duck in your hand. Hold it over the sink. Now pour the other cup of water over its back. Which statement best describes what happens to the water this time?

      a. The water sinks into the duck, just like it did the sponge.

      b. The water rolls right off the duck's back and into the sink.

6. Did the duck's weight changed in response to having water poured over it? Circle the word that best describes its weight now.

      Heavier   Lighter   About the same

MORE TO THINK ABOUT

It's no secret that kids can be cruel. Sometimes, their words and actions—or even their silence—can feel like a cold bucket of water being dumped on your head. When this happens, it is helpful to remember that you have 2 basic **CHOICES**:

1. You can choose to act like a *sponge* that soaks up the hurt and becomes weighed down.

2. You can choose to act like a *duck* and let hurtful behaviors roll off your back as you keep on swimming.

It's not always easy to act like a duck. Hurtful actions by others are not easy to ignore. There *is* an important time and place to show your true feelings about being bullied. *But the heat of the moment is never the right time.*

One thing we know about kids who bully is that they want to get a big reaction from their targets. When they see that they can hurt someone and make them feel heavy and weighed down, they feel **P**owerful. When they feel powerful, they are more likely to bully again and again.

On the other hand, when you show that you can laugh it off in the moment and just keep on going about your day, you don't give away any of your power. The person who tried to bully you will move on. He or she now knows you are too strong to be bullied.

Make it a habit to "act like a duck" whenever you face bullying.

WRITE ABOUT IT

Tell about a time when you, or someone you know, acted like a sponge in the face of bullying. What happened in the moment? What happened later?

✏️

_____

_____

_____

_____

_____

_____

Tell about a time when you, or someone you know, acted like a duck in the face of bullying. What happened in the moment? What happened later?

✏️

_____

_____

_____

_____

_____

_____

WHAT ADULTS NEED TO KNOW

The duck and sponge metaphors taught to young people through this hands-on, sensory experience are among the best, most enduring social-emotional learning tools I have ever used with young people. With my students (and with my own children), the question "Will you be a duck or a sponge in this situation?" has become a powerful language shorthand for cueing kids to carefully consider their response to a situation and to choose to respond in a way that makes their situation better.

As kids learn to choose whether they want to act like a "duck" or a "sponge" in a given situation, they gain an understanding that the outcome of that situation rests in their own hands. What's more, by making a conscious choice to "act like a duck," they retain their personal Power and become less likely to be victimized in the future.

TIPS TO HELP KIDS UNDERSTAND THE ACTIVITY

- Assist kids in obtaining a rubber duck, household sponge, water, and use of a sink in order to bring this memorable sensory experience to life for them.
- For younger kids, it can be helpful for adults to demonstrate the pouring of the water on the duck and the sponge first, then to let them recreate the experiment on their own.
- After carrying out the hands-on process, challenge kids to describe aloud what happened to the water each time it was poured.
- Encourage kids to relate the absorption of the water into the sponge—and its resulting heaviness—to what happens when kids take the words and actions of a bully to heart.
- In contrast, help kids see how, by letting the water (i.e., cruel behavior) of a bullying situation roll off its back, the duck keeps its feathers unruffled and is able to keep on swimming.

- Encourage kids to share their "Write About It" examples. Help kids contrast the outcomes of the occasions when they acted like a sponge with the times when they acted like a duck.
- To tie this activity in to the previous ones, ask kids what part of the brain they think sponges typically use and what part is most often relied upon by ducks.
- Ask kids to think about how they can act more like a duck in future situations. Explain that the next Activity in their book will teach them dozens of strategies for keeping calm and swimming on, just like a duck would do.

ACTIVITY 24 QUIZ TIME:
What Is Your Chill Out Level (COL)?

While it's natural for young people to get riled up (and feel like a sponge) during a conflict or to want to strike back at the people who hurt them, the Activities in this section of their *Activity Book* help them understand that reacting in anger almost always makes situations worse. In Activity 24, kids learn strategies to stay calm, *chill out*, and swim like a duck after a bullying incident.

WHAT KIDS LEARN

Most kids can name the things that make them feel upset. But many don't know how to chill out when they are stressed. How do you relax after a fight with a friend? What makes you feel calm after reading a mean post online or finding out that your friends all went to a party without you?

The next game will help you find your Chill Out Level (COL). You will learn ways to stay calm when bullying and other stressful things happen. Remember: Your pre-frontal cortex (*logical brain*) can do its job only when you stay calm and cool!

What's Your COL?

Directions: PART 1:

First, use the space below to think of ideas for keeping calm after a stressful incident with a friend. Write down as many ways as you can think of.

My List of Ways to CHILL OUT:

1. *Take 5 deep breaths.*   4. _____

2. _____   5. _____

3. _____   6. _____

Next, use the lines below to challenge someone else to write down their answers to the same question: "How do you chill out after a stressful incident with a friend?" Lines are provided so that their answers can be written in your book.

A Friend's List of Ways to CHILL OUT:

1. *Have a drink of water.*   4. _____

2. _____   5. _____

3. _____   6. _____

Scoring for PART 1:

a. Give yourself **1** point for every idea you came up with.

b. Give yourself **2** extra points for every idea you thought of that was not on the other person's list.

c. Tally your score. Write it in the space marked "My COL Score So Far."

My COL Score so Far: _____

PART 2:

Check out the list of ways to chill out on the next page, then turn to page 137 for final scoring directions.

50 WAYS FOR KIDS TO **CHILL OUT**

1. Go for a walk

2. Talk to an adult you can trust

3. Take 5 deep breaths

4. Squeeze a stress ball

5. Count to 10 slowly

6. Count backward from 10

7. Blow bubbles

8. Have a drink of water

9. Talk about it with a good friend

10. Ask for a hug from a friend

11. Pet a friendly animal

12. Hug a stuffed animal

13. Draw

14. Color

15. Hum a tune softly

16. Sing your favorite song in your head

17. Listen to music

18. Stop and think before saying or doing anything

19. Find a way to laugh about what happened

20. Spend some time outside

21. Practice yoga

22. Bounce a ball

23. Throw a ball

24. Go for a run

25. Think of happy or funny things

26. Remind yourself that it's OK to be upset

27. Remind yourself that it's never OK to hurt others

28. Say to yourself, "I can handle this"

29. Write about what is bothering you

30. Write a letter to someone you love

31. Read a good book

32. Do something kind for someone else

33. Go to a quiet place

34. Pray

35. Wrap yourself in a warm blanket

36. Take a warm shower

37. Relax the muscles in your face

38. Touch something soft or smooth

39. Smell something vanilla or lavender

40. Taste something yummy

41. Listen to the silence

42. Look at a photo of a loved one

43. Take a nap

44. Say "I love you" to someone special

45. Say the alphabet slowly

46. Let sand flow slowly between your fingers

47. Crumple paper

48. Eat a crunchy snack

49. Drink a cup of tea

50. Be proud of yourself for choosing a smart response!

Final Scoring Instructions:

1. Read through the list of **50** Ways for Kids to **CHILL OUT.**

2. Give yourself **5** points for each idea on your list that is not included in the **50** Ways for Kids to **CHILL OUT.**

3. Write down your score below, then try to answer the Bonus Question before learning your COL.

COL Score Now: _____

 **QUESTION:**

What do all the **50** Ways for Kids to **CHILL OUT** have in common? Write your answer in the space provided:

_____

_____

The answer to the Bonus Question can be found at the end of this activity. Check it out now, then return to this page to write down your Final Score in the space below.

My Final COL Score _____

What Is My COL?

Use your Final Score to determine your COL:

0–5 points: CUP OF TEA

You are learning to take time to calm down. This will help you to respond well to bullying and other stressful situations. Keep exploring new ways to *chill out* and cool down.

6–20 points: COLD LEMONADE

You know lots of ways to chill out and calm your brain. Because of this, you have many good choices for responding to bullying. Add any new ideas from the list of ways to *chill out* to your list of skills. This way, you will always be prepared to handle bullying.

Consider using what you know to help other kids deal with bullying. Whenever you see kids being cruel, step in to stop it. Encourage the other kids to keep a cool head and choose helpful responses.

20+ points: FROZEN SMOOTHIE ON THE BEACH

You know how to stay cool as a cucumber, no matter what kinds of bullying you face. Adults know they can count on you to stay calm and make good choices when you are stressed. Kids look up to you because you never seem to let your feelings get the best of you. Kids who bully avoid picking on you because they know that you don't allow them to have power over you.

Being respected by others is a privilege, so use your power wisely. Speak up for others who are being bullied. (See more on how to do this later in your Activity Book!) Be an example of showing kindness to everyone, every day.

WRITE ABOUT IT

Think about a time when you were the target of bullying. It may have been physical, verbal, or relational bullying or cyberbullying. In the space below, write down a plan for how you could relax and keep calm if this happened again. Include as many ways to chill out as you can. Give details.

After you have made your plan, share it with a friend, parent, or trusted adult. Ask that person to help you stick to your plan anytime bullying happens. It is helpful to connect with someone who can stay calm and help you use your logical brain. Two heads are better than one!

_____

_____

_____

_____

_____

_____

_____

⠿➡BONUS QUESTION ANSWER

All of the **50** Ways for Kids to **CHILL OUT** have one thing in common:
They give your amazing brain time to STOP AND THINK. Using your logical brain will help you make good choices when you respond to bullying.

Give yourself **10** additional points if you got the Bonus Question correct!

WHAT ADULTS NEED TO KNOW

Very often, caring adults respond to the emotional expressions of young people by saying things like, "Don't worry about it" or "You're fine. Don't let it get to you!" While these statements almost always come from a place of concern and represent the adult's earnest desire to "fix the problem" for a young person, their impact is often quite the opposite. Platitudes such as these fail to acknowledge the depth of a young person's emotions and fall short of "fixing" anything. Rather, they tend to make kids feel misunderstood and dismissed.

Rather than telling kids not to feel badly about a situation or encouraging them to deny their emotions altogether, adults are most helpful when they teach kids how to deal with the feelings they are experiencing in healthy, constructive ways. Building a young person's *COL* by teaching and role-playing multiple strategies for maintaining calm is an invaluable and lifelong gift.

TIPS TO HELP KIDS UNDERSTAND THE ACTIVITY

- Adults are encouraged to open up dialogue with kids, using open-ended conversation prompts such as:
  - ◊ How do you relax after a fight with a friend?
  - ◊ What makes you feel calm after reading a mean post online or finding out that your friends all went to a party without you?
  - ◊ Do you use different strategies to keep calm after an argument with a family member? Why or why not?
  - ◊ What are your top three most effective *chill out* strategies?
  - ◊ Were there any strategies on your friend's list that are brand new to you? If so, which ones? Do you think these strategies could be effective for you?

◊ Are there any items on the *50 Ways for Kids to Chill Out* list that you believe would not be effective for you? Explain.

- Assure kids that the effectiveness of *chill out* strategies is highly individual and that what works for one person might not work for another.
- Also, kids need to know that a strategy that has worked in the past may not be as effective in the future, depending on the nature of the bullying incident. For example:
  ◊ A young person might successfully blow off steam by going on a run (strategy 24) after a basketball practice in which a teammate repeatedly belittled her playing, but running might not be a good way to deal with her emotions after finding out her friends made plans to go to the movies but did not invite her.
  ◊ To soothe these feelings of exclusion, she may find it more calming to spend time with friends who help her feel good about herself (strategy 30).
- Encourage kids to connect this activity to the previous one in this section by asking questions such as:
  ◊ Why is it necessary to thoroughly calm down before responding to a stressful incident with peers?
  ◊ How much time do you typically need to devote to calming down before your brain is ready to respond in logical, effective ways?
  ◊ If you use a *chill out* strategy but still feel very emotional and reactive, are you ready to respond effectively? What should you do instead?
  ◊ #32 on the list says "Do something kind for someone else." How could this help you calm down?
    - Teach kids that a chemical in the brain, called serotonin, is released everytime a person commits an act of kindness. Serotonin is nicknamed "the happy hormone" because of how it relieves stress and lifts a person's mood.
- Hint: Encourage kids to plan to use more than one *chill out* strategy, especially in a highly stressful situation.

ACTIVITY 25 Friendship Emojis ☺

If you have been anywhere near a smartphone or social media site lately, you are familiar with small, eye-catching images used to convey anything from feelings to foods and weather forecasts to moods. As the old saying goes, *a picture is worth a thousand words*; in the language of today's youth, very often the picture says it all. In this activity, kids gain the opportunity to explore their emotional responses to bullying as they create and design original emojis.

WHAT KIDS LEARN

Below is a list of 7 "feeling words." They describe emotions often felt by kids who have been bullied. For each one, draw your own emoji that expresses the feeling behind the word.

FEELING WORD	EMOJI
ANGRY	
CONFUSED	
LONELY	
EMBARRASSED	
INVISIBLE	
SAD	
SCARED	

The words listed in the activity above are just a start! There is no end to the emotions you might feel about being bullied.

KEY POINT

The first step in dealing with emotions is to name them. *Naming feelings is very important. Any time we use language to describe emotions, we move them from our emotional brain to our logical brain. This way, we gain control over them.*

In the space below, make your own list of words to describe feelings you have had. Think about how you have felt with healthy friendships as well as with bullying. For each word, create an emoji to represent the feeling.

FEELING WORD	EMOJI

WHAT ADULTS NEED TO KNOW

Another important bit of neuroscience that is helpful for adults to be aware of is that the pre-frontal cortex is the part of the brain responsible for language (Dubuc, 2002). This means that while the limbic system is processing intense feelings of anger, sadness, embarrassment, fear, and so forth related to bullying, it does not have the simultaneous ability to produce the words and language needed to make sense of and express these feelings.

This activity is specifically designed to help young people put language to emotion—using the fun of popular emojis—so that they can move their processing of the bullying event from their emotional brain to their logical one and thereby improve their ability to respond effectively.

TIPS TO HELP KIDS UNDERSTAND THE ACTIVITY

- On the surface, this seems like a purely fun activity for kids. Below the surface, however, this engaging, creative task is also a powerful opportunity for kids to explore the range of emotions they experience as a result of bullying and then to put language to these emotions in order to process them effectively.
- For young children, explaining the brain science behind the activity is not necessary. Simply allow them to enjoy the creative outlet and use it as a springboard to talk about feelings. (Guidelines provided below.)
- For older kids, using age-appropriate terms to teach how talking about emotions helps their brains make good choices for responding to bullying can be both enlightening and empowering.
- Encourage kids of all ages to share the emojis they designed for the seven feeling words provided in their *Activity Book*. Challenge kids to talk about their thoughts in designing each image.

- Ask, "Was it difficult to put a picture to any of the feeling words? If so, which ones? Why?"
- If you are doing this with a group of students, challenge them to share and compare the emojis that they created in this section. Lead a discussion on the similarities and differences between the images that were created for identical words.
- Open a dialogue with kids about the "More to Think About" section, in which kids come up with their own feeling words and emojis. Ask kids to talk about a time when they felt each feeling and to explain the emoji they designed to go with it.
- In a group setting, allow young people to individually share at least one of their original feeling words and emojis and to explain the thought that went into its development.
- Come up with a new feeling word related to bullying that has not yet been shared. Challenge group members to work together to design an emoji that represents the feeling. Allow them time to talk about the feeling itself and talk with each other about the components of an emoji that would properly represent it.

ACTIVITY 26 What to Do When a Friendship Is Over

The friendships that young people form throughout the school years can be so close and so fun that kids have a hard time imagining ever *not* being close with their BFF (best friend forever). And yet when it comes to childhood friendships, the only thing that is constant is change. In this activity, kids learn to value the positive parts of a friendship but also to move on from them—when the time is right—with grace and dignity.

Moreover, Activity 26 is designed to empower kids with the knowledge that as scary as a "friendship breakup" may feel, the truth is that *they are strong enough* to handle whatever happens with their peers. What's more, *they are smart enough* to know when a friendship is no longer healthy and to acknowledge that it has become anything but fun!

WHAT KIDS LEARN

Has your BFF ever "forgotten" to save you a seat on the bus? Has your friend tackled you extra hard in football or thrown a ball right at your face? As you learned at the beginning of this Activity Book, there are times when friends are rude. There may even be days when they are very mean. But it's different when these actions become a **P**attern of ugliness. It's important to know when to say to yourself, "Enough is enough. I deserve better." Sometimes you need to end the friendship for your own well-being.

This is easier said than done! First of all, it's confusing when the person who used to be your best friend is now treating you badly. Most of us are quick to give our BFFs a second and third (and fourth and fifth and eleventh) chance. We're usually all pretty slow to admit to ourselves that things aren't getting any better. Also, it's really embarrassing to be ignored, taunted, and hurt by the person you counted on to pay attention to, include, laugh with, and have fun with you. Throw in feelings of anger, loneliness, and maybe fear—and you've got a really tough situation!

ADVICE NEEDED!

If you have ever struggled to figure out which is worse—staying with a friendship or leaving it—then you are not alone!

Directions:

Read the real-life stories of kids looking for advice on what to do when a friend becomes a "frenemy." Then, read the advice given to the kids by trustworthy adults. Finally, add your words of wisdom on how to end the friendships with dignity.

Situation 1:

Jonny, Jake, and Ethan have known each other since they were in preschool. They were best friends throughout elementary school. In middle school, however, they started growing apart. Jake and Ethan were starters on the football team. Jonny only got playing time during the second half, if his team was already winning. Jake and Ethan never invited Jonny over anymore.

At the beginning of the school year, Jake and Ethan teased Jonny in a funny way about keeping the bench warm in football. By November, the teasing started to get more cruel and embarrassing. Jake and Ethan got everyone on their team to call Jonny "Waterboy," since he was more likely to get water for the players than to play on the field. When Jonny confronted them about getting everyone to call him "Waterboy," Jake said, "Dude, relax. It was just a joke! No one knew you'd be such a loser about it."

Jonny had never felt so alone. His older brother noticed how upset Jonny was one night and asked him about it. Jonny told him what had been going on all fall. This is what his brother told him:

> **BROTHER:** Listen, bro. Friendships in middle school can be rough! Everyone says it's the girls that are so awful, but believe me—the guys can be just as bad. It stinks that this is happening to you, but I'm really glad that you finally told me about it because trying to handle this all alone is even worse. I've been through things like this with my friends, and I've got your back with Ethan and Jake.
>
> **JONNY:** Thanks, dude. I know I probably sound really stupid, but I just don't get what I ever did to them.
>
> **BROTHER:** If you did do something to them, they should tell you what it was and not just treat you like this. Friends don't just ditch friends without giving them a chance to hash it out. I'll bet you didn't do anything at all—it's just Jake and Ethan trying to climb up the school social ladder and pushing you down on their way up. It doesn't say anything bad about you, but it does tell you a lot about them. You know what I mean?
>
> **JONNY:** I guess. But why now? We've been friends forever.
>
> **BROTHER:** Trying to figure out other people's reasons for doing things is hopeless. Jake and Ethan might not even know why they're doing what they are doing. Let's just figure out what you can do to make your own situation better and not worry too much about them.

JONNY: OK. So, what should I do?

BROTHER: First, let me tell you what you shouldn't do! Never let Jake and Ethan get you upset in front of other people. No matter what they say, try to keep your cool and laugh things off. When they call you "Waterboy," come up with something funny to say back instead of getting mad. They're looking for a reaction from you. When they don't get one, they'll get bored and move on.

JONNY: Yeah, but it's so embarrassing. I hate it when they call me that!

BROTHER: I know that and you know that, and it's OK to hate the name. But you've gotta show them that you're not vulnerable to what they're saying. Be strong and confident in front of them. Laugh things off. Act like you could care less about what they say. It'll make all the difference, I promise you.

JONNY: OK, what else?

BROTHER: So, the other thing that works for me is just staying really positive. Keep your distance from Jake and Ethan when you can. Try to focus on the kids in your classes. Have you met any cool people to hang out with in any of your classes?

JONNY: Yeah, there is a pretty cool girl in homeroom named Aimee and a few guys in football that I knew from my old team.

BROTHER: Perfect. Here's my advice for you:

- Eat lunch with Aimee sometimes.
- Hang out with the other guys at football.
- When Ethan and Jake do approach you, look them in the eye so they know you are strong.
- Talk to them in a calm voice.

- Resist the urge to show them you're upset. Don't lose eye contact, agree with their put-downs, or insult them back.
- Try to find something funny to say.
- As soon as they start to be mean, change the subject or walk away.
- Focus on the kids who make you feel good about yourself.
- Move on from Ethan and Jake without sinking to their level.

What other advice would you give Jonny about handling Jake and Ethan?

_____

_____

Situation 2:

STUDENT: I invited Nikki to my party. As soon as she got there, she started making fun of everyone and everything. She told me that one of the other girls I invited was a loser. She said that I'd better be careful or people would start thinking I was a loser too. She said my dress was "hideous." I explained that my mother had made it and that I didn't like it much either but felt I had to wear it. She started telling everyone I was too poor to buy clothes. She was bossing me around, and when I wouldn't do what she told me to do, she started texting another friend of ours, telling her how lame my party was.

COUNSELOR: It never feels good to be let down by another person. We care about our friendships. It can feel so good to belong that sometimes we don't even realize that a friend is no longer good for us. It took real courage for you to talk to me about what happened. I am proud of you.

STUDENT: Thanks. I thought you were going to tell me to go back to class and handle it on my own. I guess this is all just really stupid.

COUNSELOR: Feelings are real. They are not stupid and you don't have to handle them on your own. It's important that you always surround yourself with people you can go to when you need help.

STUDENT: I am totally not talking to Nikki anymore!

COUNSELOR: What I want you to keep in mind is that the way you go about distancing yourself from Nikki is important and will say everything about the type of person you are. Here is some of my advice for you:

- Don't get into ugly wars of words with her, then half apologize by saying you were "just joking." That will only bring you down to her level.
- Resist the urge to talk badly about her to other friends—in person, online, by text, or in any way, shape, or form.
- In fact, don't put much of your energy on her at all. Shift your focus to what is going right in your life. Focus on the friendships and activities that make you feel good about yourself.
- Think about what you are doing and who you are with when you are your "best self," then plan your day accordingly. It might not be smooth sailing the whole way through, but if you keep it classy on your end, you'll free yourself up to find better friendships.

What other advice would you give this student about handling Nikki?

_____

_____

Situation 3:

Connor auditions for the school play and is offered a great role. Rehearsals are scheduled for every day after school, so Connor has to choose between hanging out with his friends and accepting the role. He chooses to do the play. Almost right away, his friends start making fun of him. They say things like, "So, are you going to have to wear tights for your role, Romeo?" and "Acting is so gay. Why do you want to be in a gay play? Are you gay or something?" Connor laughs at first, then tells the guys to "knock it off." But when one friend writes the word "gay" on his locker, Connor has had it.

What advice would you give Connor? (*Suggestions are provided at the end of the Activity.*)

_____

_____

WRITE ABOUT IT

In the space below, write about a real-life bullying situation that you know about or are involved in.

_____

_____

_____

_____

_____

- Share this situation with a trustworthy friend or adult. Ask for their advice on how to handle it.
- Talk over various options. Consider the pros and cons of each one.
- If you are involved in the situation, make a plan for how you will use the advice in your real life.
- Set a date to check back in with the friend or adult on how the advice worked out.

WHAT ADULTS NEED TO KNOW

It is not at all uncommon for young people to be at a complete loss for how to handle a personal peer conflict while still possessing an abundance of practical and credible advice for friends who are going through similar situations. Indeed, it can be hard for people of all ages to see the forest for the trees. Sometimes, supportive advice from a friend is just what we all need to find our way through the wilderness of relationships. By design, this Activity gives kids the opportunity to advise others on how to cope with bullying as a pathway to developing insight into solving their own struggles.

There are also many powerful ways that adults can support kids through the pain and confusion they feel over a "friendship breakup." In the space below, you'll find five of the most helpful things you can do for kids struggling with changing friendships:

1. **Make time**
   Not all young people want to talk to adults about friendship problems their feelings of confusion, embarrassment, and even shame. Whenever a child does confide in you, it is critical that you make the time to listen—even when it is not convenient. Especially when it is not convenient.

2. **Listen well**

   As adults, we put a lot of pressure on ourselves to have the magic words and the right answers to quickly solve kids' problems. The bad news is that kids' friendship struggles are complicated and not easily amenable to simple solutions. The good news is that young people often say that they just wish an adult would listen without giving advice. Young people are not so much looking to be fixed as they are wanting to feel heard.

3. **Keep your words kind**

   Resist the urge to say whatever mean thoughts may be going through your mind about the other kid. When you condemn a child's former friend—and then two days later they become BFFs again—things can get awkward. Even if everything you said was spot on and the child took comfort in your well-intentioned words at the time, you may well get bumped out of the confidant seat when the friendship is back on track—and you don't want that.

4. **Teach kids about change**

   Adults play a key role in helping kids understand the inevitability of change in interpersonal relationships. Remind kids that a friendship breakup is not a failure, but rather a predictable, although painful, part of growing up. Just as kids' bodies, interests, and hobbies are changing over time, so will their friendships—and that's OK!

5. **Don't take it personally**

   It is not uncommon for young people to lash out against loved ones when friendship struggles are at their worst. If a child takes his pain out on you, be willing to look beyond his behavior in the moment and empathically tune in to what is really driving his hurtful words and actions. Don't take anything a child says personally, but do remember how desperately he needs your support at this time.

TIPS TO HELP KIDS UNDERSTAND THE ACTIVITY

- Encourage kids to talk about each of the three provided situations. Specific issues to explore with young people include:
  - ◊ Kids who bully often try to downplay their actions when confronted about them. Role-play effective ways to respond to predictable justifications such as:
    - "It was just a joke."
    - "You're being too sensitive."
  - ◊ In Situation 1, what does Jonny's brother mean when he advises, "It doesn't say anything bad about you, but it does tell you a lot about them. You know what I mean?"
  - ◊ What other advice would you have given to Jonny about handling Jake and Ethan?
  - ◊ In Situation 2, what does the counselor mean when she says, "Create distance with dignity"?
  - ◊ What other advice would you have given to the student about how to handle Nikki?
  - ◊ Have you ever gone through a "friendship breakup"? What happened? How did you create distance with dignity? If you could have a do-over of your situation, would you do anything differently? Explain.
- Below, you will find key ideas about Situation 3 for your reference. This information is also provided in the *Activity Book* for young people who are using the book independently or prior to processing the activity with adults.

Discussion of Situation 3

Connor:

A very common way that boys (and some girls) put each other down is to use the word "gay" as an insult. It is very important that Connor knows that this type of name-calling is not OK and that he does not have to handle it on his own. Anyone giving Connor advice should tell him to:

- Use a *Mean-It* response, such as, "It's not cool to use that word as an insult" or "Do you even know what 'gay' means?"
- Respond with a *Mean-It* phrase and strong voice. This is often enough to end anti-gay name-calling.
- Reach out to a trustworthy adult and report the bullying if the boys don't stop using the word "gay" as an insult. Most schools have rules against anti-gay bullying. Teachers get training on how to end this type of bullying without life getting worse for people like Connor.
- Focus on the new friends he is meeting in the theatre and enjoy being in the play. When he is surrounded by people who like the same things he does, Connor can feel good about himself and how he chooses to spend his time.

To truly be a support for young people, it is essential that *Companion Guide* readers prepare themselves to respond well to bullying related to sexual orientation and identity. According to a nationwide survey, young people reported fearing anti-gay harassment more than any other kind of name-calling (Dake, Price, & Telljohann, 2003). Adults must be ready, willing, and capable of teaching kids skills to cope with this kind of bullying if they encounter it as well as to consistently confront anti-gay aggression whenever they see, hear, or become aware of it.

ACTIVITY 27 "I Took It Out on Someone Who Didn't Deserve It"

In this empathy-building exercise, young people are challenged to consider how their actions impact others. Using a hands-on, insight-oriented activity as well as a brief writing task, kids gain a new understanding of how many people are actually affected when emotions like anger and frustration are acted out on others.

WHAT KIDS LEARN

Think carefully: *Have you ever taken your bad mood or frustration out on someone who didn't deserve it?* Maybe you had a rough morning at home and took it out on some kid on the bus? Maybe school was terrible and you took it out on your little sister at home?

Let's face it: We've all misplaced a mood or two. But have you ever stopped to think about how your actions affect the person you are being cruel to? Or about how that person may then pass on his frustration to the next person he sees? *How many people are actually affected when emotions like anger and frustration are acted out?*

"IT ALL STARTED WITH BRIAN"

Directions:

Read "It All Started with Brian" below. Using the line of paper dolls, tell how each person in the story is affected by the actions of the last person in line.

"It All Started With Brian"

Brian made fun of Michelle for wearing a "loser shirt" to school. Michelle felt embarrassed. At lunch, Michelle took her feelings out on Tonya by not letting her sit with the group. Tonya sat alone and felt left out. On the bus ride home, Tonya ignored her little brother, Matthew, when he tried to sit down next to her. When their mother asked the kids how their day went, both kids brushed past her. Matthew shouted, "Just leave me alone!"

Brian	Michelle	Tonya	Matthew	Matthew's Mom
PROBABLY FEELS:	PROBABLY FEELS:	PROBABLY FEELS:	PROBABLY FEELS:	PROBABLY FEELS:
GRUMPY				

KEY POINT

In this situation, we don't know if Brian was taking a bad mood out on Michelle, if he was bullying Michelle, or if he was just trying to make a (lame) joke. What we do know, though, is that his spur-of-the-moment words had a lasting, bad impact on several other people! It's important for all of us to remember that *our words matter*—not only to the person we speak them to, but to others on down the line.

WRITE ABOUT IT

Use the paper dolls below to show a time when you said or did something hurtful to one person that caused a painful chain reaction.

_____

_____

_____

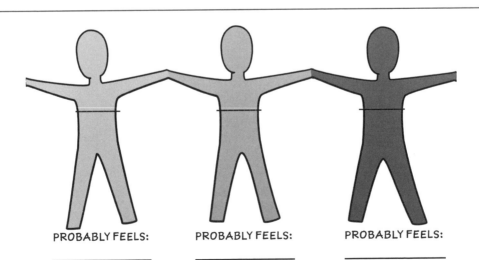

PROBABLY FEELS: PROBABLY FEELS: PROBABLY FEELS:

_____   _____   _____

WHAT ADULTS NEED TO KNOW

Kids who bully often get caught up in the social rewards they receive from their behavior (e.g., a sense of power and control over others, increased peer attention, greater social status) and lose touch with the hurtful impact their aggression has on their victims (Whitson, 2014). Activities such as this one, designed to promote empathy, give kids an understanding of how even a single act of unkindness can impact several (unintended) victims. What's more, young people are led to be more mindful of the impact their behavior has on others.

TIPS TO HELP KIDS UNDERSTAND THE ACTIVITY

- Ask kids to define the word "empathy." Depending on their ages, adults may need to introduce the concept for the first time or simply refine a young person's existing understanding of it. Empathy is also defined for young readers in the Glossary of the *Activity Book*.
  - ◊ A helpful way to talk about empathy with kids of any age is to describe it as the skill of "walking in someone else's shoes" and seeing the world from their perspective.
  - ◊ Encourage kids to understand that trying to understand someone else's thoughts and feelings is a great way of understanding—or even predicting—their behavior.
  - ◊ Challenge kids to talk about why having empathy for the thoughts and feelings of others is an important skill for having a friend, being a friend, and preventing bullying.
- Because empathy is a complex social-emotional skill, young readers will likely benefit from working side by side with an adult to consider the various ways that Brian's actions effect Michelle—and so on down the line. Older readers may more easily complete the activity independently but can still benefit from processing each subsequent turn of events with an adult.

- Encourage kids to share the situation they describe in the "Write About It" activity and to explain aloud how each person's actions impact the next.
- Challenge kids to broaden their empathy skills even further by asking them to consider more than one possible outcome of one person's behaviors on another. For example:
  ◊ In the first scenario, when Brian made fun of Michelle's shirt, Michelle took it personally and, in turn, excluded Tonya at lunch. But, what might have happened if Michelle had acted like a "duck" (see Activity 23) and made a choice not to let Brian's comments bother her?
  ◊ Or, what could have been the result of Michelle getting so upset that she made a choice to physically respond to Brian's teasing by punching him?
  ◊ Help kids think their way through several alternative outcomes.

ACTIVITY 28 Taking a New Perspective

This activity explores the wise saying "There are two sides to every story" in order to continue building the social-emotional skill of empathy in young people and to demonstrate that each human being sees the world from a unique perspective. Willingness to see someone else's point of view is an important bullying prevention skill because it strengthens mutual understanding and builds friendships. Using an intriguing, visual activity, kids learn to make it a habit to try to understand someone else's perspective.

WHAT KIDS LEARN

In the space provided below, write down the type of animal you see when you look at this image:

I see a: _____

Now, look at the image again. Try to see a different animal in the image. Write down what you see in the space below:

I also see a: _____

If you are having trouble seeing a different animal, don't worry. It can be hard to see something new once your eyes have focused on the original animal. Ask a parent, sister, brother, or friend if they can help you see a different animal than the one you have written above. Once you have found it, you may move on to the next section.

WRITE ABOUT IT

NOTE: Companion Guide readers are provided with six questions and their correct responses below. In the Kids' Activity Book, an Answer Key is provided at the end of the Activity.

Based on the picture on the last page:

1. Is this a picture of a duck? (Circle one.) (Yes)   No

2. Is this a picture of a rabbit? (Circle one.) (Yes)   No

3. How is it that both answers can be correct? Explain:

Depending on how you look at the picture, it can show both a rabbit and a duck. Often, 2 people can see a situation completely differently and both be 100% correct.

4. In the space below, draw a picture of a situation in which 2 people see something completely differently—and yet are both right.

Any picture that shows at least 2 points of view about one thing is correct!

5. How could being able to see from a new point of view help build a friendship? (Circle all that apply.)
   (a.) Kids like it when people listen to them and try to understand their point of view.
   (b.) Sometimes, being kind is more important than proving that you're right.
   c. Building a friendship is not as important as winning an argument with someone.
   (d.) When I listen to someone else's point of view, I can learn new and valuable things.

6. What is the best way to communicate with someone else when their point of view is different from yours? (Circle one.)
   a. Raise your voice until they know that your way is the only right way.
   b. Try to make the person feel stupid for their point of view.
   (c.) Ask the person questions about their point of view to try to learn more.
   d. Say nothing at all; everyone can have their own opinion.

WHAT ADULTS NEED TO KNOW

Activities focused on empathy development play a critical role in bringing an end to bullying when they teach kids to understand each other as human beings with unique needs, wants, perspectives, and feelings rather than as dehumanized pawns in a popularity game. Effective empathy development activities such as this one guide kids to be consistently mindful of how their peers are thinking and feeling. Guidelines for three additional empathy development activities are provided in Key 5 of 8 *Keys to End Bullying: Strategies for Parents & Schools*.

TIPS TO HELP KIDS UNDERSTAND THE ACTIVITY

- *Companion Guide* readers are encouraged to participate actively in this sensory activity.
- Provide encouragement to young people who struggle to see more than one "interpretation" of the duck/rabbit image. Avoid directly instructing kids how to view each image initially; however, do not allow a young reader to struggle with the task to the point of overwhelming frustration or loss of interest in the activity.
- Encourage kids to talk about:
  ◊ A real-life situation in which two people saw a situation completely differently—and yet were both correct.
  ◊ How the ability and willingness to see the world from someone else's point of view relates to conflict and bullying.
  ◊ What they think is the best way to communicate with someone whose perspective is different from their own.
  ◊ What benefits it could bring to kids to make it a habit to try to understand someone else's perspective in a disagreement or conflict.
- Two additional dual-perspective images are provided below to encourage further exploration and discussion with kids:

DISCUSSION STARTERS FOR IMAGE 1:

1. What is the first thing you see when you look at this image? Describe it.
2. Are you able to see a second image? HINT: It helps to know cursive writing.
3. Are you able to see both images at once?
4. How does the word in this image relate to the feeling some people have when they are unwilling to try to understand someone else's perspective?

Source: http://www.anopticalillusion.com/2012/06/liar-face-illusion/

DISCUSSION STARTERS FOR IMAGE 2:

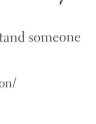

1. What is the first thing you see when you look at this image? Describe it.
2. Are you able to see a second image?
3. Are you able to see both images at once?
4. How does understanding someone else's point of view first help you know how to explain your point of view?

Source: http://mathworld.wolfram.com/YoungGirl-OldWomanIllusion.html

- A quick Internet search can provide you with many other dual-perspective images to share with young people. *Companion Guide* readers are strongly encouraged to download and discuss additional images with kids, as this is a fun and compelling way to teach kids an invaluable bullying prevention concept.

Be Known for Being Kind

ACTIVITY 29 10 Things to Say and Do to Stop Bullying

Studies show that bystanders are present during nine out of every 10 incidents of bullying but stand up for those being bullied less than 20% of the time (Hawkins, Pepler, & Craig, 2001). The same studies indicate that when young people do step in to stop bullying, however, the episode usually stops within 10 seconds.

Kids—often even more so than adults—play *the* decisive role in bringing an end to bullying. Adults—who are connected to kids—play a vital role in teaching kids how powerful they truly can be in making a difference in a peer's life.

In this Activity and the three that follow, *Activity Book* readers learn practical, effective strategies for standing up for anyone, anytime they know bullying is happening.

WHAT KIDS LEARN

Has a parent or teacher ever challenged you to stand up for a brother, sister, or classmate? Have you ever agreed that this would be a really great idea—if only you knew what to do or say?

If you answered yes to either question, you are not alone! Many kids say they'd like to stand up for people who are being bullied but don't know how. The good news is that standing up for others is probably a lot easier than you think! In fact, the simplest things you do are usually the best.

Below, you will find a list of 10 things that you can do to stop bullying anytime you see it. Then, you will add to the list by writing down simple actions and phrases to help a friend in need.

10 THINGS TO SAY AND DO TO **STOP BULLYING**

1. **Stand with the person**

   Walk over and stand next to someone who is being bullied. Often, just being there can change the mood and stop the bullying. It also lets the person being bullied know that he is not alone.

2. **Use a Mean-It statement**

   Say something like, "Cut it out, dude—that's not cool," in a *Mean-It* voice.

3. **Change the subject**

   Stop bullying in its tracks by changing the subject. For example, ask if someone knows the date of the math test or the score of the football game.

4. **Scatter the crowd**

   Say something like, "Guys, we've gotta get to class before the bell rings." This is a quick and easy way to stop bullying on the spot.

5. **Show kindness**

   If you can't stop the bullying in the moment, talk to the person later that day. Invite her to hang out with you at lunch or sit with you on the bus.

6. **Use humor**

   Try to lower the stress of a bullying situation by making kids laugh. Just make sure they are not laughing at the person being bullied!

7. **Be a connector**

   Connect a person who gets bullied with an older kid who will be his friend and tell other kids not to pick on him.

8. Get help

Reach out to a trustworthy adult who will stop the bullying

9. Reach out

Reach out to a kid you saw being bullied. Tell her you are sorry about what happened to her.

10. Be a friend

Tell the kid being bullied that he is awesome and doesn't deserve to be treated badly. This simple act of friendship can make a big difference to him.

Now, it's your turn to add to the list. How can you show kindness and support to someone who is being bullied? In the space below, think of at least 2 more ways that you can step in to stop bullying and stand up for someone who needs a hero.

_____

_____

KEY POINT

Many kids don't know how and when to stand up for someone who is being bullied. This Activity Book is designed to give you skills to safely help others and stop bullying anytime you see it.

In this Activity, you learned 10 Things to Say and Do to Stop Bullying. In the next 3 Activities, you will learn more about WHAT to say, WHEN to say it, and HOW to become known for being kind.

WHAT ADULTS NEED TO KNOW

In 8 *Keys to End Bullying: Strategies for Parents & Schools*, I explore in detail why many otherwise kind and caring kids choose to look the other way during incidents of cruelty and bullying. Three of these reasons are briefly summarized in the section below.

1. *Someone Else Will Do It:*
   In schools and other group settings, young people often believe that "someone else" will intervene in a bullying situation and thus they do not need to do so themselves.

   Companion Guide readers play a critical role in encouraging kids not to wait for others to intervene and to understand that stopping bullying is their personal responsibility.

2. *I Don't Want to be Next:*
   One of the most common reasons kids don't stand up for victims of bullying is because they fear becoming the next target of the child who bullies. During an age span when young people feel intense pressure to fit in, standing out on purpose can have negative consequences.

   To be genuinely supportive, adults must understand the real and perceived risks that kids take when they intervene and consistently equip kids with realistic strategies for intervening safely.

3. *I'm Torn Between Friends:*
   Sometimes kids feels torn about what to do during an episode of bullying, especially if one of their friends is the person dishing out the cruelty. Bystanders may think to themselves, "I don't like what she is doing, but she is my best friend," then make the decision not to intervene based on this loyalty. Helping kids find ways to surmount this

pressure and assert themselves in all relationships is another key role of helping adults.

Cultivating empathy is also especially helpful for countering the "I'm torn between friends" fears of young people. Even if they are not personal friends of a victim of bullying, a bystander must feel empathy for his or her pain and understand that this victim does not deserve to be mistreated. Consider what you can do to help your young person feel a genuine connection with and empathy for kids who are bullied.

It is important for adults to be aware of the factors that prevent young people from standing up for their peers and to take an active role in helping kids overcome these barriers to intervention. This task begins with adults acknowledging that intervening can be intimidating but can be successfully accomplished when adults show kids how to intervene safely without sacrificing their own well-being.

Both this *Companion Guide* and the *Activity Book* provide activities, ideas, and strategies to help young people overcome obstacles to intervention, empowering kids with realistic, effective, safe strategies for reaching out to their peers before, during, and after incidents of bullying.

TIPS TO HELP KIDS UNDERSTAND THE ACTIVITY

This Activity is the first of four in this section designed to empower young people with practical, effective, realistic skills for standing up for peers who are bullied.

- Use the following discussion questions to encourage kids to think about their powerful role in stopping bullying:
  ◊ What did you think when you read that other kids are present during nine out of every 10 incident of bullying but intervene less than 50% of the time?

◊ How does it make you feel to learn that when kids do intervene, the bullying usually stops in less than 10 seconds?

◊ Have you ever intervened in a bullying situation? What happened?

◊ Looking at the list of *10 Things to Say and Do to Stop Bullying*, what strategies on the list look most realistic to you? Explain.

◊ Are there any strategies on the list that would be challenging for you? Describe what would make this intervention difficult.

◊ Have you ever watched someone else stand up for a kid who was being bullied? What happened?

◊ What are your fears when it comes to standing up for someone who is being bullied?

• Spark an open-ended dialogue with your child about the common obstacles to intervention described in the "What Adults Need to Know" section. Ask:

◊ What are some of the reasons you may have chosen *not* to stand up for someone who was being bullied in the past?

◊ Have you ever *not* intervened because you hoped "someone else would do it"? Did anyone else step up?

◊ In Activities 11 through 13, you learned skills for responding effectively to conflict and bullying. How can using a *Mean-It* voice and *Mean-It* words help you stand up for others in a way that helps them and does not put you at risk of being bullied?

◊ In Activity 28, you learned about seeing from someone else's perspective. How could seeing from a bullied person's point of view help you when it comes to finding the courage to stand up for him or her?

◊ What would you do if it were your close friend who was acting like a bully to someone that you barely knew? Would it make a difference if the bullied person was someone you didn't like very much?

◊ How will you consistently find the strength to stand up for what is right, even if your friendship or personal feelings get in the way?

◊ If you were being bullied, how would you want a bystander to reach out to you?

- Reassure kids that they are not alone in worrying about the personal repercussions of standing up for others.
- Empower kids by emphasizing that the skills they are learning in their Activity Book can help them overcome the obstacles to intervention.
- As a lead-in to the next activity, ask kids to talk about when they believe is the best time to stand up for someone who is being bullied. Explain that in the next Activity, they will learn strategies for intervening anytime—before, during, and after bullying has occurred.

ACTIVITY 30 Before, During, and After Ways to Stop Bullying

In Activity 29, kids learned powerful ways to stand up for someone who is being bullied. They also learned that stopping bullying does not have to be complicated, but rather that the simplest things young people say and do can make the biggest difference in the life of someone who really needs their kindness. In this activity, kids take their new knowledge to the next level by considering the *timing* of their actions.

WHAT KIDS LEARN

Have you ever felt badly that you missed your chance to stop bullying? Maybe you didn't change the subject when a kid was being picked on in the locker room. Or maybe you didn't make space at the lunch table for someone who was being left out. If so, cheer up! *There is no bad time to stand up for someone who is being bullied.*

All of your words matter. Anytime is better than no time when it comes to showing kindness.

In the next few pages, you will read 3 bullying situations. For each case, you will think about what you could do before, during, and after to help the person being bullied.

Before, During, and After Ways You Can Help

Directions:

Read each real-life situation below. Write down at least 3 things that you could do to be a hero to the person being bullied. Challenge yourself to come up with an idea that can be used:

1. *Before* the bullying in order to prevent it
2. *During* the bullying to stop it on the spot
3. *After* the bullying to support and comfort the person who is bullied.

Situation 1: Jessie & Kris

Jessie is mad at Kris. She thinks Kris has been flirting with her boyfriend. Jessie doesn't want to say anything to Kris about it because she doesn't want to fight. Instead, Jessie makes a fake website about Kris. She uses all sorts of embarrassing photos and posts. Jessie gets other kids to post videos on Kris's wall. They all post about how they hate Kris and what a loser she is. In no time, the whole school seems to know about it.

WHAT COULD YOU DO TO HELP KRIS?

Before: _____

During: _____

After: _____

Situation 2: Darrell & the Bus Kids

Darrell dreads his bus ride home from middle school. Every day, the kids who sit behind him slap him on the back of his head. The kids who sit in front of him turn around to shout bad words. They tease him, asking, "What are you gonna do, cry to your mama?" One kid threatened to beat him down if he told anyone at school about what happens on the bus. Darrell has tried to get his parents to drive him home from school. They both work and can't change their schedule. This has been happening for months.

WHAT COULD YOU DO TO HELP DARRELL?

Before: _____

During: _____

After: _____

Situation 3: Chloe & Olivia

Chloe and Olivia have been best friends since kindergarten. In 3rd grade, they are put in different classes. Each girl makes new friends. All is fine at the beginning of the school year. But then, later in the year, Chloe starts to say things to Olivia like, "You're not my best friend anymore" and "You can't sit with me at lunch. This table is only for my new friends." One day, Olivia walks into the school cafeteria and finds that no one in the whole grade will sit with her. Everywhere she tries to put her tray down, kids say the same thing: "This table is only for cool kids. You are not one of them."

WHAT COULD YOU DO TO HELP OLIVIA?

Before: _____

During: _____

After: _____

Before, During, and After Ways You Can Help

A N S W E R   K E Y

There are many ways to stand up for kids before, during, and after bullying. Compare the ideas below with the ones you wrote down. Remember that you can always CHOOSE how you respond to bullying. Make yourself known for being someone who always chooses kindness.

SITUATION 1: JESSIE & KRIS

BEFORE:

- Refuse to post embarrassing videos or rude comments.
- Alert a teacher.
- Warn Kris about what is happening so she can stop it before it spreads further.
- Prevent the problem by telling Jessie that Kris is not flirting with her boyfriend.
- Encourage Jessie to talk to Kris and tell her why she is mad.

DURING:

- Take screen shots of the cyberbullying. Report it to an adult.
- Remind Jessie that what she is doing could get her in a lot of legal trouble.
- Tell Jessie that the website she made is not funny. Tell her to take it down right away.
- Refuse to take part in the cyberbullying.
- Tell others not to take part in the cyberbullying.
- Reach out to Kris as a friend. It is likely that she is feeling ganged up on and alone.

AFTER:

- Be there as a friend for Kris.
- Include Kris in activities and at your lunch table.
- Encourage Kris to get an adult's help.
- Offer to go with Kris to talk to a teacher, school counselor, or parent.

SITUATION 2: DARRELL & THE BUS KIDS

BEFORE:

- Invite Darrell to sit with you on the bus.
- Sit with Darrell near the front of the bus, closer to the driver.
- Talk to the bus driver in private to let him or her know what is happening.
- Request assigned seats on the bus to protect Darrell from the kids who are bullying him.
- Ask your parents to talk to Darrell's parents about what is happening on the bus.
- Tell a trustworthy teacher at school about what is happening to Darrell on the bus.

DURING:

- Use a Mean-It voice to tell the kids on the bus to "knock it off."
- Make your voice loud enough to get the bus driver's attention.
- Sit with Darrell on the bus. Help him to laugh or play a game.
- Ask a respected older student to sit with Darrell on the bus.

AFTER:

- Call Darrell after school. Tell him you are sorry about the way the other kids treat him.
- Tell Darrell that he does not deserve to be treated that way.
- Remind Darrell that you like him.
- Arrange for a group of nice kids to sit with Darrell on the bus ride from now on.
- If your parents ever drive you to school, offer Darrell a ride.
- Talk to a trustworthy teacher at school who can help address the situation.

SITUATION 3: CHLOE & OLIVIA

BEFORE:

- Refuse to go along with the crowd that is being cruel to Olivia.
- Tell Chloe and the other girls that what they are doing to Olivia is not cool.
- Get a bunch of your nicest friends to sit with you and Olivia during lunch.
- When you hear Chloe's plan to leave Olivia out at lunch, make up a believable reason to sit at a different table that day. Save a seat for Olivia at that table.

DURING:

- Refuse to go along with activities that exclude Olivia.
- Make a joke out of Chloe's statement that "only cool kids" sit at the lunch table. Use humor to distract everyone while making space for Olivia to sit.
- Start a new conversation at the table. Talk about a school event, holiday, or any subject that distracts from Chloe's cruel plans.
- In a Mean-It voice, tell the mean girls at lunch that "cools kids don't treat people that way."

AFTER:

- Talk to a teacher or lunch aide about the way Olivia is being treated.
- Text Olivia after school. Invite her to hang out with you and your friends.
- Help Olivia think of some Mean-It comebacks she could use next time Chloe and the other girls are cruel.

WHAT ADULTS NEED TO KNOW

Along with all their academic lessons during the school years, kids are learning how to use social power. Professionals and parents have a vital role to play in teaching kids just how powerful they are—that the actions they take before, during, and even after an episode of bullying can make a real difference in whether the cruelty stops short or continues mercilessly. For kids, the basic message is clear: If you know that bullying is happening, you have the power and you own the responsibility to do something to stop it.

TIPS FOR HELPING KIDS UNDERSTAND THE ACTIVITY

- Adults can be extremely helpful to kids by processing each of the situations provided in this Activity. Use the suggested Before, During, and After interventions for each situation to facilitate conversation. Keep in mind that the ideas provided in the Answer Key are just a start; *Companion Guide* readers and kids will likely have additional ideas, all of which are valid as long as they focus on supporting the bullied person without directly putting down or harming the child who bullies.
- Encourage kids to talk with you about each individual situation and to relate each one to their own personal experiences. When necessary to enhance insight and understanding, add in your own encounters with bullying and helpful bystander interventions.

ACTIVITY 31 50 Kind Words and Phrases to Stop Bullying

Throughout this Activity Book, young people learn that the words they use (and the tone of voice they choose) really matter when it comes to bringing an end to bullying. In this Activity, kids gain a vocabulary of 50 encouraging words and phrases that they can use to help others before, during, and after an incident of bullying. The *50 Kind Words and Phrases* list can be photocopied, bookmarked, or even carefully torn out of the *Activity Book* so that young people can refer to it readily for helpful things to say during moments of conflict and bullying.

WHAT KIDS LEARN

Have you ever seen someone else hurting, but not known what to say to help them feel better? This activity will help make sure you are never again at a loss for kind, encouraging words.

Directions:

On the next page, you will find a list of 50 Kind Words and Phrases. These are things you can say to someone before, during, or after they are bullied. (Or you can say them anytime a person needs a bit of kindness!) Read the whole list and circle the 10 words and phrases you are most likely to use.

50 KIND WORDS AND PHRASES

1. You are awesome.

2. Do you want to sit with me on the bus today?

3. Let's sit together at lunch.

4. I'll text you after school.

5. I know you can handle it.

6. You are strong.

7. You are a great friend.

8. I'm so sorry she said that to you. That wasn't right.

9. You didn't deserve her cruelty.

10. You've got this.

11. I understand.

12. I've been there.

13. Me too.

14. You handled that so well. I'm impressed!

15. I don't know if I could have done that as well as you did. Good job!

16. How did it go?

17. Let me know how it goes.

18. I know you'll do great.

19. Don't give up, no matter what.

20. I've got your back.

21. I'll be there for you no matter what.

22. Don't pay any attention to what they say.

23. You rock.

24. Is there anything I can do to help you?

25. Try not to take it personally.

26. Who cares what anyone else thinks? What matters is what you think!

27. Text me and let me know what happens.

28. I'll cross my fingers for you.

29. Good luck!

30. Do you need to talk?

31. I believe you.

32. I believe in you.

33. Believe in yourself!

34. I think you should tell a teacher about what just happened. If you want, I'll go with you.

35. Would you mind if I tell a teacher about what just happened?

36. How did you do that?

37. I'm excited to see what you do.

38. I know you're going to do great.

39. I like hanging out with you.

40. It's fun to do things with you.

41. I'm glad you're here.

42. I'm happy to talk with you.

43. Do you want to hang out after school?

44. I'll walk you home from the bus.

45. I'll meet you after class and go with you to your locker.

46. I'm listening.

47. I'm here for you.

48. You make me laugh.

49. You're the best.

50. You're my BFF.

WEEKLY LOG

Over the next 7 days, keep a record of the kind words and phrases you say to others. In the space provided, write down WHAT you said, WHY you said it, and HOW the other person responded.

EXAMPLE:

DAY I:

I said: *"I'll walk you home from the bus."*

Because: *A few kids in our neighborhood kept teasing Jenna on the bus.*

He/ she: *Smiled at me and said, "Thank you!" She seemed relieved.*

DAY 1:

I said: _____

Because: _____

He/she: _____

DAY 2:

I said: _____

Because: _____

He/she: _____

DAY 3:

I said: _____

Because: _____

He/she: _____

DAY 4:

I said: _____

Because: _____

He/she: _____

DAY 5:

I said: _____

Because: _____

He/she: _____

DAY 6:

I said: _____

Because: _____

He/she: _____

DAY 7:

I said: _____

Because: _____

He/she: _____

I'm with you.   You're the best!   You can do it

Great job   Awesome!

WHAT ADULTS NEED TO KNOW

Kids learn in Activities 21 and 22 that when confronted with a stressful situation such as bullying, their limbic system is activated. This emotional part of their brain is responsible for the "deer in headlights" phenomena, where kids freeze up and can't think of anything helpful to say.

By helping kids develop a practical vocabulary of encouraging words and phrases, *Companion Guide* readers enable them to more quickly overcome the brain freeze induced by bullying and to access helping words even in a stressful situation. The more opportunities kids have to practice saying encouraging words aloud, the better prepared they will be to use them when they see a peer in need. Use role-play, discussion, and review of the Weekly Log as ways to make the *50 Kind Words and Phrases* part of a young person's everyday vocabulary.

TIPS TO HELP KIDS UNDERSTAND THE ACTIVITY

- Pause to consider the types of words and phrases you typically use with young people. Are you an encourager? How will you role-model the types of supportive messages that you want young people to use to build each other up?
- Ask kids to share with you the 10 words and phrases from the list that they are most likely to use. Challenge them to talk about why they feel particularly comfortable with these phrases.
- Ask: "What original words and phrases did you write down? Are these words you use often? When or with whom do you use these encouraging phrases?"
- Encourage kids to talk about a time when they supported a friend in need with encouraging words, such as those on the list. What impact did their words have?
- Ask kids to share a time when someone used a word or phrase from the list

to reach out to them when they were being picked on or bullied. How did the kind words make them feel?

- Challenge kids to talk about a time when they witnessed a bullying situation in which no one stepped in to say or do anything to support the victim. Ask kids to reflect on the incident:
  - ◊ Why do you think no one stood up for the bullied person?
  - ◊ What kind of intervention could have been effective?
  - ◊ Knowing what you know now, what would you do to reach out to the person being bullied?
  - ◊ What would have been the best timing for an intervention—before, during, or after the incident?
  - ◊ What kinds of encouraging words might have helped the person?
  - ◊ What would you have wanted someone to say or do if the bullied person in the situation had been you?

- Use role play to give kids practice in using encouraging words with a person who is being bullied. Remember, the more practice kids have saying the words and phrases aloud, the more they will be able to access the words during a stressful moment.

- Ask kids about the experience of logging their kind words and phrases for seven days:
  - ◊ Describe the experience of recording your supportive words for a week.
  - ◊ Did you feel like you helped anyone? How?
  - ◊ Did keeping a daily log of your words make you more likely to say kind things to others this week?
  - ◊ Were there certain words and phrases you used more often than others?

- Adults are challenged to keep their own log of the kind messages they speak over the course of one week and to share the log with young people as a way to encourage dialogue and reflection.

ACTIVITY 32 What's Your Tagline?

In the first three activities of this section, kids learn that standing up for someone who is bullied can be:

1. Easy

Use any of the 10 Things to Say and Do to Stop Bullying (pages 167–168) to stand up for anyone you see being bullied.

2. Timeless

Anytime is a good time to reach out to a person who is being bullied. You can say or do something before, during, or after bullying to be a hero to someone who needs your help.

3. Kind

Look back on your Weekly Log (pages 179–181) to see how many people you can help by saying kind words. Words matter a lot! Your kind words will help a bullied person feel supported and less alone.

In this Activity, kids are taught a fourth fact about standing up for those who are bullied; they learn that these easy, timeless, and kind acts are:

---

4. Your responsibility!

Read on to find out more.

WHAT KIDS LEARN

Standing up for someone who is being bullied starts with you. Yes, YOU! You might be hoping a parent or teacher will do something about the problem. Or maybe you think someone who is better friends with the person being bullied will step in. Perhaps you are just crossing your fingers and hoping that the bullying stops on its own.

Forget any of these "Someone else will stop it" options!

If you know that bullying is happening to someone else, YOU have the power and the responsibility to do something to stop it.

So, what will you do to stop bullying anytime you are a witness to it?

Tell The World Your Tagline

Directions:

1. Come up with your own phrase (or borrow one below) that best describes your role in standing up for others. Examples of good taglines are:

- Be Known for Being Kind
- Stopping Bullying Starts with Me
- It Only Takes One
- Bullying Stops Here
- I M Here 4 U
- Keep Calm & Stop Bullying

2. Write down your tagline here: _____

3. On the next 2 pages, design a T-shirt that tells your bullying prevention tagline to everyone you meet. Be as creative as you'd like! Use color, designs, or even texture to make your tagline stand out!

WHAT ADULTS NEED TO KNOW

As school-age children move into their tween and adolescent years, developmentally they are exploring their identity. Often, this process is akin to the floor of a young person's closet—littered with personalities that were "tried on" like a new pair of pants, but then judged as "not a good fit" and so discarded in place. *Companion Guide* readers can serve as a "mirror" of sorts to young people who are trying on different identities for size—by reflecting affirmation of their good choices (such as showing kindness and standing up for others) and encouraging further examination of questionable decisions (like posting hurtful comments online or failing to support a friend in need.)

This activity taps kids' creative sides by giving them the opportunity to design their own T-shirt and, in the process, communicate their identity in stopping bullying. Do they want to be known for being kind? Can peers count on them to be loyal? Brave? Strong? What does their tagline say about how they will handle a bullying situation?

TIPS TO HELP KIDS UNDERSTAND THE ACTIVITY

- This is a powerful, fun, and memorable activity for kids of all ages—even those who think that they "don't like art." More than a craft or drawing task, Activity 32 provides kids with the opportunity to think about their identity and role in stopping bullying and to communicate it proudly to others.
- Encourage kids to share their T-shirt designs and taglines with others. How did they come up with their tagline? What do they hope to communicate through this brief personal statement?
- What does the color, pattern, and/or texture of the shirt design (if any) add to the message of the tagline?
- *Companion Guide* readers are encouraged to help creative young people take Activity 32 to the next level by providing them with a T-shirt and fabric markers (or other craft supplies) that they can use to actually make their own bullying prevention tagline T-shirt.

Reach Out to Kids Who Bully

ACTIVITY 33 Everyone Has a Story

In this Activity, readers are provided with two real-life bullying scenarios and asked to consider what might possibly be going on in the world of the aggressive young person to make him or her act out with such cruelty. This is an empathy development exercise in which kids learn that *every person has their own story* and that stopping bullying often starts with understanding the background events in the life of any young person.

WHAT KIDS LEARN

Read each situation below. Then use the space provided to answer questions about the story of the person who bullied.

Situation 1

What witnesses saw:

Jada and Liza were playing together at recess. They were laughing and skipping and chatting. All of a sudden, their classmate, Riley, ran up behind them. Riley grabbed one end of Liza's scarf and started pulling on it so that Liza turned around to face her. Then, quick as a flash, Riley grabbed the other end of Liza's scarf. She crossed it around Liza's neck and started to choke her! Liza was stunned. Jada called out for help. Two recess aides arrived and pulled Riley off Liza. Riley was sent to the Principal's office. Her parents were called to pick her up. She was suspended from school for 5 days.

Based on what the witnesses saw:

1. Who do you think acted like a bully? _____

2. Who do you believe was being bullied? _____

3. Do you think Riley's punishment was fair? _____

What most people didn't see:

For the last 4 school days, Jada and Liza had been taunting Riley. They had been making fun of her during class, at lunch, and during recess. Each day, they would make fun of the horse stickers on her notebook. They would taunt her about how food got stuck in her braces. At recess, they kept making promises to play with her, but then they would run away every time she got near them. On Friday,  Riley found out that Jada and Liza had been writing love notes to a boy named Ollie, pretending that they were written by Riley. Riley was embarrassed when all of Ollie's friends laughed in her face at recess.

Feeling hurt and angry, Riley tried to catch up with Liza to ask her what was going on with the notes. Riley kept calling Liza's name, but Liza did not turn around. To get Liza's attention, Riley ran up behind her and grabbed the end of her scarf to get her to turn around. Liza looked at her and said, "Oh, look! It's Ollie's girlfriend!" Jada laughed out loud. At that point, Riley got so mad that she grabbed the other end of Liza's scarf. Before she even knew what she was doing, she was pulling the ends around Liza's neck. The next thing she knew, 2 recess aides were screaming at her and she was being marched to the Principal's office.

Now that you know more of the story:

1. Who do you think acted like a bully? _____

2. Who do you believe was being bullied? _____

3. Do you think Riley's punishment was fair? _____

4. How did your point of view change when you learned the whole story?

_____

_____

_____

Situation 2

What witnesses saw:

Kyle was a quiet kid who usually kept to himself. But every time he got frustrated, he would take out his feelings on his classmates. One day, he couldn't understand the math lesson. He called the kid sitting next to him a "butt-face loser." Another day, a girl cut in front of him in the lunch line. He shoved her and knocked her tray to the floor. Her food spilled everywhere. Last week during gym, Kyle felt embarrassed about being picked last. He punched one of the team captains right in the stomach.

On Wednesday, Kyle arrived late to school. His clothing was wrinkled and his hair smelled funny. He fell asleep during language arts. When his teacher went to wake him, he yelled, "Get off me, you stupid witch!" and swatted her arm. When the girl next to him laughed, Kyle kicked her desk over and yelled, "What are you laughing at, you ugly butt-face?" Kyle was sent out of class and told to go straight to the counselor's office.

Based on what the witnesses saw:

1. Who do you think acted like a bully? _____

2. Who do you believe was being bullied? _____

3. What do you think should happen to Kyle? _____

What most people didn't see:

By the time he was in 3rd grade, Kyle had already lived in 7 foster homes. His mother was in prison. He had never met his dad. This month, Kyle was living in a house with 2 other foster children. One of them was a 14-year-old boy named Christopher. Christopher was really mean to Kyle. He always took Kyle's clothes and food. He called Kyle names like "butt-face loser." Worst of all, when he got mad, he would hit Kyle and kick his things. On Tuesday night, Kyle played video games until 3 a.m. He was trying to stay awake to make sure that Christopher didn't steal any more of his things. Kyle finally fell asleep in his clothes. He woke up the next morning too late to shower, change, or even eat breakfast before school.

Now that you know more of the story:

1. Who do you think acted like a bully? _____

2. Who do you believe was being bullied? _____

3. What do you think should happen to Kyle? _____

4. How did your point of view change when you learned the whole story?

_____

_____

_____

MORE TO THINK ABOUT

It can be scary to watch bullying happen—especially in school where all kids deserve to feel safe. To be clear: **There is no excuse for violence. There is never a time when name-calling is okay.** The purpose of this Activity is not to excuse Riley, Kyle, or any kids who hurt others. But it is important to know that *what you see with your eyes is not all there is to see.*

In any situation, it is good to slow down and get information about a situation before you decide what is going on. Show that you are smart by finding out what happened *before* the bullying you saw. Share your kindness by understanding that there may be more to the situation than meets the eye.

Sometimes, you will find that the event was as simple as one person being cruel to someone else. Other times you will learn that there was a long chain of events that led up to the bullying you saw. The person who appeared guilty at first might actually be a victim of cruelty.

KEY POINT

It is important to take time to understand a person and his or her situation. Only then can you respond well.

WRITE ABOUT IT

Has anyone ever punished you for something they thought you did, without understanding the full story of why you did it? Describe the event:

- What did others see you do?
- What else was happening that these people did not know about?
- What did you learn?

_____

_____

_____

_____

_____

_____

_____

_____

_____

_____

_____

Remember, it is never okay to be cruel or violent. It is important to keep in mind that every person has a story. This is a first step in ending conflict and solving problems.

WHAT ADULTS NEED TO KNOW

This Activity challenges young people to think outside the box of traditional labeling and punishments for kids who act out aggressively and to consider what might possibly be going on in the life of the young person who behaves with such cruelty. Making time to think differently and approach others from a place of compassion is rare; most systems seek to simplify the dynamics of conflict and bullying by zeroing in on a guilty person and punishing him or her so that they feel better and can cross "intervention" off their to-do list. And yet, bringing an end to bullying is often much more complicated than a task on a checklist, and truly changing the behavior of aggressive kids requires more than reactive punishment. By discussing Activity 33 with young people, you can take an active role in cultivating the critical skill of empathy in young people and in teaching the value of seeking to understand others.

To be clear, the purpose of this Activity is not to excuse or exonerate kids who bully. Rather, Activity 33 challenges kids to begin to look beyond surface behavior to understand why certain people behave the way they do. The emphasis should be placed on having empathy and compassion for the experiences of others.

TIPS TO HELP KIDS UNDERSTAND THE ACTIVITY

Use the questions provided for each situation to begin your discussions, then encourage young people to explore additional themes from the two scenarios, including:

- What did you think about Riley when you read the first part of the situation?
- Once you read the second part of her story, did your thoughts and feelings change at all? Explain.
- Why is it important to gather all the facts about a situation before jumping to conclusions and assigning a punishment?

- Have you ever been in a situation where someone saw only one part of what happened and acted based on a limited understanding of the facts? Describe the situation and how you felt about the person who acted before gathering all the facts.
- Have you ever known a kid like Kyle?
  - ◊ Do you know anything about his or her life outside of school?
  - ◊ If so, could difficulties in the individual's personal life have caused their aggressive behavior at school?
  - ◊ Does knowing about these difficulties change the way you think or feel?
- It is very troubling to see a person like Kyle behave cruelly toward others. Is it possible to both stand up to the bullying *and* try to understand the aggressive student at the same time? Explain.
- What does this Activity teach you about the phrase *"Everyone has a story?"*

ACTIVITY 34 5 Favorite Things About Me

This activity is designed to build self-esteem in kids and counteract the harshness with which some youngsters treat each other. Readers are challenged to create a list of the things they love most about themselves. In the process, they learn how celebrating their strengths can keep them strong and resilient in the face of bullying.

WHAT KIDS LEARN

What could a **5 Favorites** list of things you love about yourself have to do with stopping bullying? Before moving on, write down your answer to this question in the space below:

_____

_____

As you learned way back in Activity 1, kids who bully are often trying to build up their own **P**ower. Feeling powerful can be a great thing. But when kids build themselves up by pushing others down, it's like a real-life game of Whack-a-Mole that has no winners!

One of the best ways to bring an end to bullying is to take so much pride in yourself and have so much confidence in your abilities that no one can push you down.

Some kids worry that taking pride in themselves is like bragging. The 2 things are definitely different! Use this simple chart to know the differences between taking pride in yourself and bragging to others:

TAKING **PRIDE** OR **BRAGGING**?

YOU ARE TAKING **PRIDE** IN YOURSELF IF:	YOU ARE **BRAGGING** IF:
You talk about trying hard and being the best you can be. **Example:** *I practiced for an hour every single night to learn that song on the piano. I'm so happy the hard work paid off.*	You talk about how easy it is to be so much better than other people. **Example:** *I barely practiced at all and I still did better than anyone else at the piano recital.*
You encourage yourself and others at the same time. **Example:** *Our team was awesome today! There was so much good passing and scoring by all of us.*	You lift yourself up by pushing others down. **Example:** *Did you see how many times Jonny fumbled the ball? It's his fault we didn't get that touchdown. Good thing I was there to score the winning touchdown!*
You celebrate your own strengths. **Example:** *Art is my best subject.*	You compare yourself to others. **Example:** *I'm the best artist in the whole school.*

Now you understand how pride is different from bragging. You know that being proud of who you are can even protect you from the effects of bullying. It's time to get started on your **5 Favorites** list!

Directions:

On page 201, write down 5 of the best things about you. The only catch is, you are NOT allowed to list items related only to how you look. So, for example, you should AVOID writing down something like:

1. I love my long legs.

OR

2. My red hair is so fabulous.

On the other hand, you CAN list how your body helps you do something or how a trait makes you unique, such as:

1. I love that my long legs help me to run very fast.

OR

2. I feel special that I am the only person with red hair in my whole grade.

KEY POINT

Try your best to focus your **5 Favorites** list on your inner qualities—traits like kindness, loyalty, and being a good listener. These are the traits that help you connect with others. They help you become even stronger in the face of bullying.

5 FAVORITE THINGS ABOUT ME

1. _____

2. _____

3. _____

4. _____

5. _____

CONGRATULATIONS on completing your **5 Favorites** list. But wait; you are not done yet!

Building self-confidence does not happen overnight. Writing down 5 things you love about yourself *today* will not help you unless you read the list *tomorrow*—and the *next day*—and the *day after that* . . . and so on. Staying strong in the face of bullying is not a single event, but rather an everyday activity. Your **5 Favorites** list is meant to be just the beginning.

To take this activity to the next level, try at least one of these Bonus Challenges:

1. Use a phone to film yourself reading your **5 Favorites** list aloud. This video is not to be posted online or viewed by anyone else. This recording is simply for you— to watch every day to remind you of your best qualities. Watch it whenever you need an extra boost of confidence.

2. Read the list aloud to a parent, brother, sister, or other relative. It may feel embarrassing at first, but hearing their comments on your strengths can help boost your pride and confidence even more. Maybe you'll even inspire someone you love to create their own **5 Favorites** list!

3. Repeat the **5 Favorites** list aloud while looking in the mirror. Do this each day for the next 10 days. You will likely feel awkward at first. By Days 8, 9, and 10, though, you may notice that your words feel more true and your strengths sound real. You may realize that you are far too confident to let anyone else bring you down.

WHAT ADULTS NEED TO KNOW

For many young people—both boys and girls—body image plummets during the tween years (Drexler, 2015). Areas of perceived weakness are often exploited by peers who seek to elevate their own social status by pushing others down. Activity 34 encourages young people to zero in on at least five things that they love about themselves and to truly value those things, rather than focusing on faults or believing others' put-downs.

Companion Guide readers have a vital role to play in helping kids develop and maintain a positive self-image through their childhood, tween, and teen years. Your feedback can make a huge difference in affirming the positive things that a child highlights about herself through this activity.

TIPS TO HELP KIDS UNDERSTAND THE ACTIVITY

- Encourage kids to talk about the items they wrote down on their 5 *Favorites* list. Some may feel very awkward about sharing at first, but the very act of doing so is a powerful way to build self-confidence.
- Ask kids to elaborate on specific strengths, skills, or abilities on their list.
- Challenge kids to talk about why a particular item makes them feel especially good about themselves.
- If you are discussing this activity with a group of kids, help them compare their lists and note items they have in common. This can be a great bonding experience and way to promote mutual support for specific interests and abilities.
- Ask kids to think about the purpose of the activity:
  ◊ How can recognizing and celebrating your strengths help protect you from bullying?
- Reference the "Bonus" challenges:
  ◊ Ask kids to explain in their own words why building self-esteem is not a

once-and-done activity, but rather a skill to be practiced over and over again.

◊   Challenge kids to tell you which of the bonus activities they will undertake.

◊   As you are able, provide a smartphone for kids to film themselves reading their 5 *Favorites* list, or offer to do the filming for them.

◊   Be a young person's audience as she is reading a 5 *Favorites* list aloud. Offer feedback that affirms the items on their list.

◊   As time goes by, check back in with kids about specific items on their list. For example, if a child has listed "I'm a great soccer player," be sure to check in with her from time to time on how the soccer season is going, what position she likes to play, and so forth.

ACTIVITY 35 I Am Who I Am!

In Activity 34, kids were encouraged to celebrate the characteristics, qualities, and abilities that make them strong and unique. In this Activity, kids move beyond the list of 10 top traits to create a piece of word art that captures even more of the essence of their personality.

WHAT KIDS LEARN

Most of us are many different things, to many different people. Whether or not we like acting on stage, we all play several roles in life. There is no one in the world exactly like you. This is your chance to celebrate that wonderful fact!

Directions:

Using the large "I" on the next page, create a work of art. Fill the space inside the "I" with words, phrases, emojis, or even pictures. They should describe the roles you play, the people you love, the subjects that interest you, and anything else that describes your unique place in the world.

An example is provided to help you get started thinking about the possibilities for your "I Am" masterpiece!

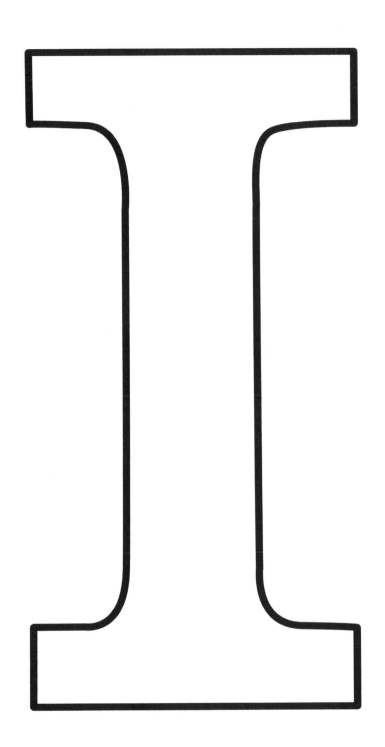

WHAT ADULTS NEED TO KNOW

The purpose of this Activity is to help readers overcome self-doubt and perceived inadequacies that can make them vulnerable to the cruelty of others. Through this visual, keepsake Activity, young people are encouraged to recognize their strengths and take pride in their many positive qualities.

TIPS TO HELP KIDS UNDERSTAND THE ACTIVITY

- *Companion Guide* readers are strongly encouraged to use the "I" provided on the previous page to create their own word art.
  - ◊ Doing so gives you a unique understanding of what kids experience as they complete the activity.
  - ◊ What's more, your completed "I Am" work of art can be shared with young people as a way to connect and encourage an active discussion of the activity.
- Invite young people to talk to you about the words, phrases, and pictures they included in their "I."
  - ◊ Ask open-ended questions to encourage kids to describe various items in detail.
  - ◊ Challenge kids to think about the difference between the first several items they wrote down and the last few. Is there a difference between these roles?
- Given that the focus of this project is on "I," it's natural for kids to think mostly about themselves as they are writing. Thinking about themselves in relation to others, however, is a critical social skill.
  - ◊ Use conversation to encourage kids to focus on how their personality, skills, likes, and interests can impact others and be used to help someone else—particularly during a situation such as bullying.

◊ For example, if a young person writes down that they are "kind to others," ask them to share an example of a time when they were kind to a friend who had been bullied.

◊ Or, if a child shares that he is "athletic," encourage him to think about how he can connect with classmates who aren't as good at sports. Often, athletes enjoy a special kind of social status in a school setting. As such, kids who excel at sports can be especially helpful in reaching out to peers who are often picked on and offering them some protection from bullying.

◊ This holds true for unlikely pairs of kids with any kind of interests. When connected with a high-status peer, vulnerable young people can often shed the target on their back and actually enjoy a measure of social success in their own right (Whitson, 2014). More information on the benefits of buddy systems in school can be found in *8 Keys to End Bullying: Strategies for Parents & Schools.*

• To wrap up the discussion, challenge kids to comment on something new they learned about themselves through this activity.

◊ Encourage kids to explore themes of the many different roles, strengths, and abilities they have and how these roles can help connect them to their peers in positive ways.

ACTIVITY 36 Would You Rather?

This activity uses the fun "Would You Rather" game format (in which players have to choose between two distinct options) to encourage young people to think deeply about friendship. Using real-life options that challenge kids to think through the differences between being "popular" and being "well-liked," readers gain insight into the types of friendships that help them feel best.

WHAT KIDS LEARN

- What is the difference between being "popular" and being "well-liked?" Write down a few words to describe each in the space below:

"Popular" means: _____ _____ _____

"Well-liked" means: _____ _____ _____

- If you had to choose, would you rather be part of a popular crowd at school or be well-liked by most people? (Circle one.)

Popular   Well-liked

- Is it possible to be both popular AND well-liked? Explain in your own words how a person can be BOTH at the same time:

_____

_____

Now it's time to have some fun. Play the **Would You Rather** game on the next page. Read some of the real-life choices kids your age face when it comes to forming friendships. You will learn about your own style for deciding what matters most in a friend.

Would You Rather . . .

Directions:

Using any color pencil or crayon, shade the choice you are most likely to make in each of the 12 situations.

1. Play a game you like with kids who are not very nice to you.	Or	Play a game you don't like with kids who are always nice to you.
2. Be the first person picked for the team.	Or	Be the first person a friend turns to when they need to talk.
3. Be invited to every classmate's birthday party this year but not hang out with any of them at school.	Or	Spend time at school each day with 2 close friends but not be invited to any other birthday parties.
4. Swim in a pool full of M&M's.	Or	Swim in a pool full of Skittles.
5. Hang out with someone who is really fun and exciting but not very kind.	Or	Hang out with someone who is really kind but also a bit boring.
6. Win a $25 gift certificate to an ice cream shop and go with a kid who is mean to everyone.	Or	Spend $5 of your own money to go out for ice cream with your best friend.

7. Be the oldest kid in your family.	Or	Be the youngest kid in your family.
8. Be known for being beautiful.	Or	Be known for being kind.
9. Play with a classmate who wears stylish clothes but insults your outfits.	Or	Play with a classmate who has no sense of style but is really adventurous and fun.
10. Hang out with a kid who owns all of your favorite video games but never lets you have a turn to play.	Or	Hang out with a kid who only owns 3 games but always makes sure you get a fair amount of time to play.
11. Be able to fly.	Or	Be able to make yourself invisible.
12. Have a friend that is nice to you in person but says mean things online.	Or	Have a friend that posts really nice things about you online but is mean to you in person.

MORE TO THINK ABOUT

Look back on your responses to the **Would You Rather** game.

IF YOU CIRCLED THE ITEMS ON THE LEFT MOST TIMES:

It is clear that being popular is important to you. You are not alone in wanting to fit in with the crowd and "be known" by all the kids. It's OK to enjoy being popular, but make sure that you don't climb your way to the top of the social ladder by pushing anyone else down. Be known for being kind always—to everyone, and not just the kids who sit at the cool table or who are invited to all the parties. Make sure that the kids you spend time with treat you well. These kids should ask you what you think, include you when they talk, respect your choices, and help you feel good about yourself whenever you are together.

IF YOU CIRCLED THE ITEMS ON THE RIGHT MOST TIMES:

You have the strength and confidence to value real friendships. It is important to you to have a few close friends that you can be yourself with. You know that it might be fun to go to a few more birthday parties. It could be cool to brag that you own all the latest video games. But you know that spending time with kids who are always kind and trustworthy is a whole lot better. Have faith in your choices. Whenever you are able to choose your friends, *choose kind.*

IF YOU CIRCLED ANY ANSWER FOR #4, #7, OR #11:

You are correct! These **Would You Rather** questions were thrown in just for fun. So, M&M's or Skittles—which will it be?

IF YOU CIRCLED EITHER ANSWER FOR #12:

This question is the hardest choice of them all. Neither answer sounds very good, does it? As you learned in Activities 14 to 20, technology can make friendships complicated! Whenever you can, *refuse to choose* between options like the ones in #12.

A friend is someone who is kind to you in person AND online. You should never have to make a choice between the two. If you find that a kid acts one way online and a totally different way in person, it's time to use your skills from Activities 12 and 13 to tell this person how you feel about what they are doing. If the person keeps treating you badly, use your skills from Activity 26 to move away from this friendship with dignity.

KEY POINT

It's not always easy to make smart choices when it comes to friendships. Sometimes your heart tells you one thing while your brain tells you another. The great thing about a game like **Would You Rather** is that the consequences of your choices are pretty clear: Either spend time with kids who are popular but not very nice in person, or spend time with someone you can count on to be kind and fun most of the time. Which type of friendship *would you rather* enjoy?

WHAT ADULTS NEED TO KNOW

Many young people confess their desire to be "popular." Through their behaviors, some show that they are even willing to push others down to pull themselves up the school social ladder. This activity is designed to acknowledge the drive to be popular while underscoring that being popular can have real costs.

Using the either/or format of the Would You Rather game, readers learn that sacrificing time with the "in" crowd can earn them more time with genuine friends. While real life rarely presents itself in such clear, black-and-white terms, this Activity clears away the gray area for a time to help kids clearly see the consequences of their choices in friendships.

TIPS TO HELP KIDS UNDERSTAND THE ACTIVITY

- Review kids' responses to the questions presented at the beginning of the Activity so that they can talk to you in a conversational way about:
  - ◊ The differences between being "popular" and being "well-liked"
  - ◊ Their preference for being part of a popular crowd at school or being well-liked by most people
  - ◊ If and how a person can be both popular and well-liked at the same time
- Engage kids in a discussion about the items in the *Would You Rather* game:
  - ◊ Were there some questions that were easier to decide between than others?
  - ◊ Which ones were simple to decide between? Explain.
  - ◊ Which ones presented a tough choice? Why?
  - ◊ As kids look at the explanations of "left" answers vs. "right" answers, do the descriptions ring true? Why or why not?
- Challenge kids to create two to three original *Would You Rather* questions based on situations from their real life.
  - ◊ If you are talking about this Activity with just one young person, talk through the *Would You Rather* questions that he or she wrote. Encourage your young person to think through several aspects of the scenario, including various possible outcomes for each choice.
  - ◊ If you are using this Activity with a group, have kids work in pairs or small groups to "quiz" each other on their original *Would You Rather* questions and discuss their responses together. As a large group, select a few of the kid-generated *Would You Rather* questions to discuss.

ACTIVITY 37 Staying Tuned In to Others

Do you spend much of your life on the go? Is your to-do list perpetually a mile long? In a culture that glorifies "busy," adults and kids alike tend to lead very full lives, and it's easy to see how we can become transformed from "human beings" into "human doings." Tasks take up so much of our time that we sometimes become oblivious to the feelings and needs of the people around us. This fun, memorable (and tasty!) activity* is designed help young people keep others in mind, even when there's a lot going on in their lives.

WHAT KIDS LEARN

Being able to understand and share in the feelings of others is called **empathy**. The skill of empathy allows you to know how someone else is thinking and feeling because you have been through something like it in your own life. In other words, empathy helps you put yourself in someone else's shoes and see from their point of view.

When you show empathy to someone who has been bullied, you help them to feel less alone and more understood. When you show empathy for a person who has acted like a bully, as in the examples in Activity 33, you can help them understand that there are different, better choices that can be made for acting out their troubles.

This next activity gives you a great way to understand the idea of empathy. It will help you to show empathy anytime you find out about a bullying situation.

*Linda Van Voorst, "Ice + Marshmallow" activity, www.justicekids.org. used with permission

Sweet Empathy

Directions:

For this activity, you will need:

- A handful of small, sweet treats, such as mini marshmallows or M&M's
- A few ice cubes

Step 1:

Eat 2 to 3 of the sweet treats. Savor the flavor. Then, in the space below, write down a few words to describe their taste and texture (such as *sweet*, *smooth*, or *soft*).

_____   _____   _____

Step 2:

- Now, place an ice cube in your mouth. Keep the ice cube on your tongue for as long as you can—until either it melts or your mouth is so cold that you can't take it anymore.
- As soon as the ice cube is gone, place 2 to 3 of the sweet treats in your mouth. Quickly, write down words to describe their flavor now:

_____   _____   _____

Step 3:

Did you notice a difference in the taste of the sweets before and after eating the ice cube? Circle the answer that best describes what happened AFTER eating the ice:

- **a.** The sweet treats tasted the same the second time around.
- **b.** The sweet treats tasted even sweeter the second time around.
- **c.** I couldn't taste the sweets treats as well the second time around.

Discussion

- In Step 1, it should have been easy to taste the flavor of the sweet treats.
- In Step 2, however, you held the ice cube in your mouth for a while. Your tongue became frozen, or *numb*. When your tongue is numb, your sense of taste does not work for a while.
- For that reason, in Step 3 most people choose answer C: "I couldn't taste the sweets treats as well the second time around."

This is how it is with bullying!

Sometimes we get so caught up in our own busy lives or in our own thoughts and feelings that we become *numb*. Our ability to sense the feelings of others doesn't work as well for a while. One of the best ways to bring an end to bullying is to always stay tuned in to the feelings of others—both kids who are bullied and kids who bully others. When you show empathy for what is happening to others, you help them to feel better understood, less alone, and more able to make good choices in how they treat others.

WHAT ADULTS NEED TO KNOW

In the world of bullying prevention, empathy is an important skill to develop in young people. This is because kids who bully often get caught up in the social rewards they receive from their behavior (e.g., a sense of power and control over others, increased peer attention, greater social status) and lose touch with the hurtful impact their aggression has on their victims (Whitson, 2014). This experiential and sensory exercise is designed to cultivate empathy in young people as readers learn the importance of tuning in to others' thoughts, feelings, and needs.

TIPS TO HELP KIDS UNDERSTAND THE ACTIVITY

- *Companion Guide* readers can enhance this Activity greatly by making available a handful of small sweet treats as well as a few ice cubes to allow kids the full sensory experience.
- Adults are encouraged to participate in the Activity alongside kids so they can share in the sensory experience and speak more genuinely about it.
- Ask kids to reflect aloud about their ability to notice the flavor of the sweet treats before and after holding the ice cubes in their mouth.
- Encourage kids to relate this sensory experience to bullying and to taking time to tune in to the needs and feelings of their peers.
- Challenge kids to think about specific strategies for staying tuned in to others, even when their own lives are busy. It may be helpful for you to share with young people how you balance your own needs with meeting the needs of others.

Keep Talking About Ending Bullying

ACTIVITY 38 Kindness Matters

Little acts of kindness make a big difference in bringing an end to bullying. Sometimes, they make the biggest difference of all. In this Activity, kids learn the power of one word, one smile, one door held open, one invitation to sit at the lunch table, one text just to say "hi," or one high-five offered each and every day.

WHAT KIDS LEARN

Has a compliment from a friend ever brightened your rough day? Has a nod from your teacher ever given you the confidence to keep trying? Neither of those *actions* took a lot of time or cost money, but both are the types of kindness that can turn someone's whole day around. When young people make kindness cool, bullying won't stand a chance at school!

Kindness Challenge

Directions:

1. Using the worksheet on the next page, read the 20 ideas for simple, quick, and no-cost acts of kindness that you can do for others at school or at home.

2. Select 1 act of kindness from the worksheet. Your challenge is to carry out this kindness AT LEAST ONCE PER DAY, OVER THE NEXT 30 DAYS.

3. Whenever you can, carry out the act of kindness for a DIFFERENT PERSON each day. Spread as much kindness as possible!

4. Record your acts of kindness in the 30-DAY KINDNESS CHALLENGE LOG on page 215.

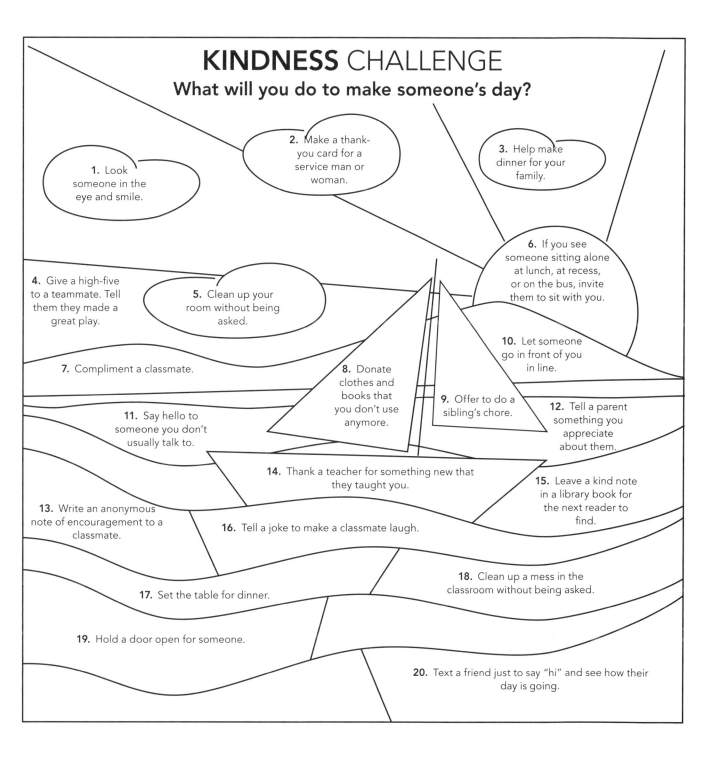

30-DAY KINDNESS CHALLENGE LOG

Record your act of kindness and who you did it for in the space provided.
If you see the person's reaction to your kindness, please note it.

✽ DAY 1	✽ DAY 2	✽ DAY 3	✽ DAY 4	✽ DAY 5	✽ DAY 6
✽ DAY 7	✽ DAY 8	✽ DAY 9	✽ DAY 10	✽ DAY 11	✽ DAY 12

✿ DAY 13	✿ DAY 14	✿ DAY 15	✿ DAY 16	✿ DAY 17	✿ DAY 18
✿ DAY 19	✿ DAY 20	✿ DAY 21	✿ DAY 22	✿ DAY 23	✿ DAY 24
✿ DAY 25	✿ DAY 26	✿ DAY 27	✿ DAY 28	✿ DAY 29	✿ DAY 30

IN ADDITION to choosing 1 act of kindness to perform each day over the next 30 days, make it a goal to *carry out all 30 of the acts of kindness listed.* Color in each shaper as you complete it.

When the entire **KINDNESS CHALLENGE** worksheet is colored, carefully tear out the page from your Activity Book. Proudly display it in your room, on the fridge, or anywhere you will see it. It will remind you that your 30 simple acts of kindness made a big difference to others.

WHAT ADULTS NEED TO KNOW

Mahatma Gandhi taught that "the fragrance always remains on the hand that gives the flower." Indeed, when young people show kindness toward their peers, they reap many personal rewards, including a greater sense of social connection and belonging (Marsh & Suttie, 2010), increased happiness and reduced stress (Hamilton, 2011), and even improved memory and learning (Currie, 2015). What's more, Dr. Kimberly Schonert-Reichl (2015), of the University of British Columbia, says that kindness creates a sense of connectedness within school communities that reduces the likelihood of bullying.

It is clear that kindness has numerous benefits and that it really does matter. *Companion Guide* readers play an important role in teaching kids to show kindness, not just as an afterthought once all of their schoolwork is complete or as merely a "fun family activity" to do once a year around the holidays, but rather though *every action, every day.* Encouraging kids to complete the 30-Day Kindness Challenge is a great way to begin making kindness a habit for your young person.

TIPS TO HELP KIDS UNDERSTAND THE ACTIVITY

- Help kids brainstorm meaningful, no-cost acts of kindness they can carry out in school or at home.
- Encourage kids to talk about ways that peers, siblings, or parents show kindness to them. Ask:
  - ◊ How do you feel when someone shows kindness to you?
  - ◊ Has a simple act of kindness ever changed your day? Explain.
- Then, ask kids to describe the way they feel when they are kind to someone else. Ask kids to describe a specific instance in which they showed kindness to someone who was not already a friend or family member and the impact that that act of kindness had on both the recipient and themselves.
- Ask kids open-ended questions to encourage reflection on the value of occasional "big" acts of kindness—such as expensive gifts—versus a "small" everyday act of kindness—such as a smile in a school hallway.
- Participate alongside your child in the 30-Day Kindness Challenge.
  - ◊ Use the log provided in this *Companion Guide* to record your own acts of kindness. Set aside a specific time each day to talk with kids about the kindnesses you acted out for others.
  - ◊ Even more than talking about what you did to show kindness, emphasize the impact that you notice your kindness had on its recipient.
  - ◊ Challenge kids to discuss Gandhi's wise quotation as it relates to kindness and bringing an end to bullying: *The fragrance always remains on the hand that gives the flower.*

ACTIVITY 39 Create-a-Campaign

In this Activity, young people are challenged to create their own bullying prevention campaign at school, complete with a schedule of events, activities, projects, and games that they think would be helpful for stopping bullying and building better relationships among students.

WHAT KIDS LEARN

October is National Bullying Prevention Month in the United States. During these 31 days, many schools and other places for kids have activities to raise awareness for ending bullying. You know how important it is to keep kids safe throughout the year. Your mission is to create a *Bullying Prevention Campaign* that lasts throughout the school year. In the space provided, plan fun activities that teach bullying prevention messages all year long.

To get you started, here is a list of common bullying prevention activities hosted by schools. Use any of these—or come up with your own ideas—to involve students and teachers in efforts to end bullying throughout the year.

COMMON BULLYING PREVENTION ACTIVITIES

- Poster contests
- T-shirt days
- Assemblies
- Author visits
- Film festivals
- Mix-it-up lunches
- Book fairs
- Walks
- Pledges

On the next few pages, plan at least one **Bullying Prevention Campaign** event for each month of the school year. Think about the main goal of your event, how many students and teachers you will need to help you make it happen, a list of supplies, and any other important details. Let your imagination run wild! Dream big. Be creative. **It is up to you to create the change that you want to see in the world.**

EXAMPLE (BASED ON ACTIVITY 38):

ACTIVITY NAME:	The **30-Day Kindness Challenge**
GOAL OF ACTIVITY:	To show that little acts of kindness make a big difference in stopping bullying
WHAT WILL HAPPEN:	Kids will think of no-cost, simple acts of kindness. They will choose 1 act to carry out each day of the month and record their **30 Acts of Kindness** in a journal.
WHO WILL HELP PLAN:	One student from each grade, along with 2 teachers to help organize students and tell the whole school about the Challenge
SUPPLIES NEEDED:	Each student completing the Challenge will need their own journal to record the Acts of Kindness for 30 days.
OTHER DETAILS:	Kids will share their journals with their teacher and classmates at the end of the 30 days.

MONTH 1

ACTIVITY NAME: _____

GOAL OF ACTIVITY: _____

WHAT WILL HAPPEN: _____

WHO WILL HELP PLAN: _____

SUPPLIES NEEDED: _____

OTHER DETAILS: _____

_____

MONTH 2

ACTIVITY NAME: _____

GOAL OF ACTIVITY: _____

WHAT WILL HAPPEN: _____

WHO WILL HELP PLAN: _____

SUPPLIES NEEDED: _____

OTHER DETAILS: _____

_____

The kids' Activity Book provides space for 9 months of event planning—enough for an entire school year.

WHAT ADULTS NEED TO KNOW

Creating cultures of kindness in schools and bringing an end to bullying are not once-and-done events, but rather a consistent series of activities that adults and kids work on together throughout all the days of the year. Hosting back-to-school bullying prevention rallies and organizing anti-bullying slogan contests during National Bullying Prevention Month (October) are both terrific ideas that get people thinking and talking about the importance of stopping unwanted aggressive behavior. But they are not enough. To be truly effective, we must keep the conversation going about bullying prevention all year long.

Often the best sources of ideas for engaging, relevant, meaningful bullying prevention activities are kids themselves! After all, young people are the true experts when it comes to knowing the ins and outs of the social dynamics of their school. Likewise, students are in the best position to understand the types of initiatives that will genuinely speak to their peers and inspire them to sincerely change bullying behaviors (Whitson, 2014).

Consider your role in supporting your child in his bullying prevention efforts at school and think about how you can help rally students and educators to engage as well. Your encouragement and support—combined with your young person's firsthand knowledge and insights—can make for one powerful team!

TIPS TO HELP KIDS UNDERSTAND THE ACTIVITY

- *Companion Guide* readers can support kids in countless ways with this Activity, including:
    ◊ Helping kids brainstorm engaging, relevant, realistic events and activities
    ◊ Encouraging kids' ideas, insights, and initiatives

◊ Role-modeling leadership skills as kids learn to direct the activities of their peers

◊ Organizing schedules for monthly events

◊ Coordinating adult and student volunteers

◊ Gathering supplies

◊ Communicating with administrators, teachers, parents, and students

◊ Informing local media about the student-led bullying prevention activities at the school

- Be aware that there will likely be a steep learning curve for young people as they learn to plan and oversee bullying prevention events for their school community. Not everything will go as planned. Not everyone will agree. It's OK. Encourage kids to learn from their mistakes, to apply corrections as needed, and to keep going with their school-changing campaigns.

ACTIVITY 40 What's Your Video Message?

This is the 40th and final Activity for kids to complete in their *Activity Book*—and it's quite a *production!* Readers are challenged to think back on the most helpful, memorable challenges, experiments, discussions, games, readings, and quizzes from the first 39 activities and to create their own two- to three-minute video to share the best of what they have learned. With the encouraging reminder that they are now *stronger, wiser, and in a better position to help themselves and others*, this creative challenge helps young readers synthesize the new knowledge and skills they have gained by completing the 8 *Keys to End Bullying Activity Book*.

WHAT KIDS LEARN

Think back on your favorite activities from this book:

- Which worksheets helped you learn something new?
- Was there a quiz that you found especially fun?
- Did the information about your amazing brain amaze you?
- Have you started using *Mean-It* phrases already?
- Did the ideas for standing up for others before, during, and after bullying help you help someone else?

IN THE SPACE BELOW, WRITE DOWN 3 OF THE ACTIVITIES YOU REMEMBER MOST:

1. _____

2. _____

3. _____

One focus in this Activity Book was on the many ways that you can use technology to have fun and be creative. In this final activity, you are challenged to do just that!

Directions:

Create your own 2- to 3-minute video that features strong, kind ways that young people can make a difference in their school, their neighborhood, or even their country to bring an end to bullying. Be creative. You may choose to highlight a piece of learning from any of the activities in this book, or you may choose to feature your own ideas. This is your chance to use your powerful voice to spread positive messages about stopping bullying.

After you have created your original video message, share it with your parents, teachers, family, and friends. The more widely you share your message, the more people will learn about helpful ways to bring an end to bullying.

WITH PERMISSION FROM A PARENT, consider sending your video message to me via email at signe@signewhitson.com. Selected videos will be posted to the *8 Keys to End Bullying Activity Book* channel on YouTube. Tune in to watch video messages posted by other kids your age. Just remember: Only positive, encouraging comments are permitted on our channel!

Kindness matters in person, online, and everywhere you go. Our community is a safe place for kids to share their messages about bringing an end to bullying.

Good luck creating your video message! I hope to see it on YouTube!

WHAT ADULTS NEED TO KNOW

It has been said that if you want a person to learn something, you should have them *read* about it; if you want a person to understand something, you should have them *write* about it; and if you want a person to master something, you should have them *teach* it. The 8 *Keys to End Bullying Activity Book for Kids & Tweens* makes use of a diverse range of teaching strategies in order to meet the needs of all readers. In this final Activity, it provides young people with the opportunity to master their new bullying prevention knowledge and skills by creating a teaching video.

The first step in creating the video is for kids to reflect on all they have learned through the first 39 Activities of their book. The value of this process cannot be overstated. As readers look back on pages they may have completed weeks or months before, they are reminded of essential facts, skills, how-to's, and personal insights that require regular refreshing in order to become a part of the young person's everyday knowledge base.

As kids sort through the lessons and prioritize which ones are most meaningful, they personalize their learning and identify specific areas for growth and skill development. Then, in planning how to convey positive, supportive messages to their peers via a video message, kids have the opportunity to crystallize their new knowledge on how to bring an end to bullying (not to mention the chance to use the technology they love in a creative and constructive way!).

TIPS TO HELP KIDS UNDERSTAND THE ACTIVITY

- Sit with your child as she looks back on completed *Activity Book* pages and identifies several of the most helpful, memorable messages. Encourage discussion about what made particular activities, games, or quizzes so meaningful.
- Brainstorm content ideas for the two- to three-minute video:

◊ What will be the main focus?

◊ How will the main idea be conveyed?

- Help your child write a script for the video.

  ◊ What do they want to say?

  ◊ How to do they want to say it?

  ◊ What will the tone be for the video? Serious? Funny? Perhaps a role-play would be a good way to teach a concept or skill?

- Encourage kids to consider various aspects of planning their video, such as:

  ◊ Who is their intended audience? Do they want to make a video for elementary school students or for middle schoolers? Or, maybe your child has a message to deliver to parents or teachers.

  ◊ How can their important message be conveyed in a two- to three-minute video?

- Give kids constructive feedback throughout the process of creating their video.

- Encourage kids to persist despite inevitable frustrations in creating their video message.

- Allow kids access to a video-recording device, such as a smartphone or tablet.

- Assist kids with filming their video message.

- Help kids edit their video (if necessary) for clarity and length.

- Encourage kids to share their video message on the 8 *Keys to End Bullying* YouTube channel. Remind young people that only positive, encouraging comments are permitted on the page.

  ◊ Watch the videos posted by other *Activity Book* users.

  ◊ Talk with kids about the content of the videos and the messages shared by their peers in other schools and locations.

- Perhaps the most important role of *Companion Guide* readers in this Activity—and throughout the book—is to help young people figure out how to make their voices heard when it comes to spreading positive messages about stopping bullying.

A Final Note

Dear Parents & Professionals:

Thank you for guiding your child or group of children through the discussions, games, and thought exercises in their Activity Book. As a caring adult who dedicates time to teaching new skills and a trustworthy confidant who helps young people feel heard and understood, you communicate that *kindness matters*, *words matter*, and—most important—*young people matter*!

The Certificate of Achievement template, provided on the following page, offers you one final opportunity to acknowledge and honor the efforts of each young person who completes the Activity Book—whether independently or as part of a bullying prevention unit or group.

Simply add the child's name and present the Certificate to him or her, along with your signature and the date. In awarding each certificate, please offer encouraging words of confidence in the young person's ability to manage bullying with competence and dignity. Last, please challenge your young person(s) to make sure that this is not the end of their Activity Book, but rather the beginning of bringing an end to bullying.

With gratitude and admiration for all that you do to nurture kids,

Signe

Signe

P.S. If you have used this *Companion Guide* to lead a group of young people through the activities, you are permitted to make photocopies of the certificate template so that each child can receive a personalized recognition of her achievement in understanding and ending bullying.

CERTIFICATE *of* ACHIEVEMENT

THIS ACKNOWLEDGES THAT

[Recipient Name]

HAS SUCCESSFULLY COMPLETED THE

8 KEYS TO END BULLYING ACTIVITY BOOK

[MONTH/DAY]
[YEAR]

Date

References

Agule, P. (2012, June 21). Liar face illusion [Image]. Retrieved from http://www
.anopticalillusion.com/2012/06/liar-face-illusion

Burke, D. (2015). There's a new cyberbullying "emoji" in town and the story
behind it is brilliant. Retrieved from http://metro.co.uk/2015/10/24/theres
-a-new-cyberbullying-emoji-in-town-and-the-story-behind-it-is-brilliant-545
9492/#ixzz3paeevM3K

Currie, L. (2015). Why teaching kindness in schools is essential to reduce
bulling [Blog post]. Retrieved from http://www.edutopia.org/blog/teaching
-kindness-essential-reduce-bullying-lisa-currie

Dake, J. A., Price, J. H., & Telljohann, S. K. (2003, May). The nature and extent
of bullying at school. *Journal of School Health, 5,* 173–180.

Drexler, P. (2013). Beauty and the boy: The impact of negative body image on
our boys [Blog post]. Retrieved from http://www.huffingtonpost.com/peggy-
drexler/beauty-and-the-boy-the-im_b_2462766.html

Dubuc, B. (2002). The evolutionary layers of the human brain. Retrieved from
http://thebrain.mcgill.ca/flash/d/d_05/d_05_cr/d_05_cr_her/d_05_cr_her
.html

Hamilton, D. (2011, June 2). 5 beneficial side effects of kindness [Blog post].
Retrieved from http://www.huffingtonpost.com/david-r-hamilton-phd/kind
ness-benefits_b_869537.html

Hawkins, D. L., Pepler, D. J., & Craig, W. M. (2001). Naturalistic observations
of peer interventions in bullying. *Social Development, 10*(4), 512–527.

Laugeson, L. (2013). Comebacks for being teased [Video file]. Retrieved from
http://www.kidsinthehouse.com/video/comebacks-being-teased

Lenhart, A. (2015). Teens, social media & technology overview 2015. Retrieved
from http://www.pewinternet.org/2015/04/09/teens-social-media-technology
-2015

Ludwig, T. (2013, February 20). How to talk to your kids about bullying [Blog post]. Retrieved from http://www.aplatformforgood.org/blog/entry/how-to-talk-to-your-kids-about-bullying

Marsh, J., & Suttie, J. (2010, December 13). 5 ways giving is good for you [Blog post]. Retrieved from http://greatergood.berkeley.edu/article/item/5_ways_giving_is_good_for_you

Marston, K. (2013, Dec. 26). Cotton vs. sandpaper words [Blog post]. Retrieved from https://theschoolcounselorkind.wordpress.com/2013/12/26/cotton-vs-sandpaper-words/

Rutherford-Morrison, L. (2015, September 2). ReThink app prevents cyberbullying by making people think twice before posting messages. *Bustle*. Retrieved from http://www.bustle.com/articles/108224-rethink-app-prevents-cyberbullying-by-making-people-think-twice-before-posting-messages

ReThink. (2015). What is ReThink? [Webpage]. Retrieved from http://www.rethinkwords.com

Schonert-Reichl (2015). Ripple kindness project: School curriculum [Webpage]. Retrieved from http://ripplekindness.org/school-curriculum/

Siegel, D. (2012). Dr. Daniel Siegel presenting a hand model of the brain [Video file]. Retrieved from https://www.youtube.com/watch?v=gm9CIJ74Oxw

Siegel, D., & Bryson, T. P. (2011). *The whole brain child: 12 revolutionary strategies to nurture your child's developing mind*. New York, NY: Bantam Books.

Van Voorst, K. (2013, December 20). "Ice and marshmallow" activity [Blog post]. Retrieved from www.justicekids.com

Weisstein, E. W. (n.d.). Young girl–old woman illusion. *MathWorld—A Wolfram Web Resource*. Retrieved from http://mathworld.wolfram.com/YoungGirl-OldWomanIllusion.html

Whitson, S. (2011). *Friendship & other weapons: Group activities to help young girls aged 5–11 to cope with bullying*. London, UK: Jessica Kingsley.

Whitson, S. (2014). *8 keys to end bullying: Strategies for parents & schools*. New York, NY: W. W. Norton.

Index

Note: Italicized pages refer to illustrations; tables are noted with *t*.